PRAISE FOR *Men on Strike*

"*Men on Strike* is an important contribution to understanding the sexual disequilibrium feminism left in its wake."

—James Taranto, *The Wall Street Journal*

"The patriarchy of feminist lore is in full retreat. Three decades of media male-bashing, father-averse family courts, and feminized classrooms have led millions of male hegemons to drop out—from education, marriage, fatherhood, and even the workplace. In this riveting and eye-opening book, Helen Smith explains how it all happened, why it is harmful, and what can be done to turn things around."

—Christina Hoff Sommers, resident scholar of the American Enterprise Institute and author of *The War Against Boys*

"*Men on Strike*'s compassion for men both psychologically and socially ranks Dr. Helen Smith as perhaps the most courageous female psychologist writing about men today. If you are a man wishing to open your heart to the possibility of being seen by a woman, Helen Smith proves it is possible."

—Warren Farrell, PhD, author of *The Myth of Male Power* and *Why Men Are the Way They Are*

"Part of what makes *Men on Strike* powerful is that Smith writes as both psychologist and journalist. As the former, she brings a wealth of knowledge gained through years of helping men and listening to their deepest struggles and fears. As the latter, she demonstrates that this subject isn't simply about feelings—the myriad problems and injustices men face have a political, legal, and material basis."

—Glenn Sacks, MA, men's issues columnist

"One of the reasons I wanted to talk to you is because so few people today have the courage in the current cultural and political climate to stand up for men."

—Rush Limbaugh, *The Limbaugh Letter*, July 2013

"It's an important book. Read it. You may disagree with her ideas, but it's hard to disagree with the trends Dr. Smith exposes. And ultimately, you cannot argue with men who aren't there."

—Shawn T. Smith, PsyD, licensed psychologist and
author of *The Woman's Guide to How Men Think:
Love, Commitment, and the Male Mind*

". . . her stance is sure to incite lively debate."

—*Publishers Weekly*

"Smith draws heavily from the actual experiences of men, using their stories and comments to illustrate the disaffection, anger, and sorrow that many feel. The anecdotes she provides—the voices of the men themselves—are powerful. . . . Smith lets us listen, and walks the reader through the ways that men's rights have been constricted. . . . Instead of blaming men and ridiculing the lifestyle of those who have 'failed to launch,' Smith explores the idea that men may be making a purposeful, even rational, choice in rejecting a society that already has rejected them. . . . Also setting Smith's book apart from other treatments of the plight of men is her advice on how they can, as individuals and as a gender group, work to restore a more balanced society."

—Carrie Lukas, "The Siege of Men,"
National Review, July 15, 2013

"However—and it can be painful to admit this—some of her premises are true. . . . Men and boys do struggle in school. They are often less able to express emotional frustration fluently. And we may owe them more support than we're currently giving them."

—Sarah Begley, "How We Fail Our Boys,"
Daily Beast, September 13, 2013

MEN ON STRIKE

MEN ON STRIKE

MEN ON STRIKE

Why Men Are Boycotting
Marriage, Fatherhood,
and the American Dream
—and Why It Matters

HELEN SMITH, PhD

ENCOUNTER BOOKS

New York • London

First American edition published in 2013 by Encounter Books,
an activity of Encounter for Culture and Education, Inc.,
a nonprofit, tax-exempt corporation.
Encounter Books website address: www.encounterbooks.com

Manufactured in the United States and printed on
acid-free paper. The paper used in this publication meets
the minimum requirements of ANSI/NISO Z39.48-1992
(R 1997) (*Permanence of Paper*).

PAPERBACK EDITION ISBN: 978-1-59403-762-7

THE LIBRARY OF CONGRESS HAS CATALOGUED
THE HARDCOVER EDITION AS FOLLOWS:
Smith, Helen, 1961–
Men on strike : why men are boycotting marriage, fatherhood, and
the American dream : and why it matters / by Helen Smith, PhD
pages cm
ISBN-13: 978-1-59403-675-0 (hbk. : alk. paper)
ISBN-10: 1-59403-675-6 (hbk. : alk. paper)
ISBN-13: 978-1-59403-676-7 (ebk.)
1. Men—United States—Attitudes. 2. Men—Psychology. 3. Marriage.
4. Sex discrimination against men. I. Title.
HQ1090.3.S65 2013
155.3'32—dc23
2012042992

*To my father, who taught me how to love, and
to my husband, for keeping his achievement alive,
and, of course, for Julia always.*

*And to the Army of Davids who
helped me put this book together.*

Contents

Contents

Preface to the Paperback Edition

Your book made me feel appreciated, understood,
and like I'm no longer walking alone.
—Christian, a reader from Massachusetts[1]

I am delighted that this paperback edition of *Men on Strike* is now available, as it means the original hardback was successful enough to warrant another round of readers for this newer version. Since the hardback edition of the book came out, I have been surprised at how many men around the country have written me to share more about their situations, and I will discuss their stories and comments below. But first, I want to address the critics of the book who say that there is no war on men, or if there is, men bring it upon themselves, or who say no hard data shows without a doubt that men are discriminated against. I don't buy this at all.

There truly is a war on men going on in our society, and the average man knows it full well. Most men may not talk about it or allow themselves to think that a "democratic" society would treat its citizens without due process or justice. Yet that is what is happening to many men in today's misandric climate, and it is proven again and again as newspaper articles and stories show men being sentenced to jail even after paying child support, men being falsely accused of rape, men being forced to pay exorbitant amounts of alimony, or men being dismissed from jobs or college over unproven sexual harassment charges. For example, a recent Houston news story told of father Cliff Hall, who paid his outstanding child support for his eleven-year-old son but was sentenced by a female judge to six months in jail anyway.[2]

After *Men on Strike* came out, numerous naysayers complained that I used too many anecdotes to explain why men did not want to marry as often, attend anti-male colleges, or interact with kids for fear of being called a pervert. Evidently anti-male sexism must be "proven" beyond a shadow of a doubt, whereas sexism against women is taken as a given though the facts may show otherwise. Misandry, the hatred of men, is so rarely discussed or investigated that most people don't know what the word means. Even sympathetic men reading my book said they seldom heard discussion of the information it contained, or the material was dismissed as tales from a bunch of evil (and probably racist!) "men's rights activists"—the only "rights activists" who get no respect in today's world.

So how do you get people to grasp where men are coming from? You educate them and help them to understand there is really a problem, and it causes suffering. I hoped that *Men on Strike* would be the catalyst to open the dialogue, and it was, given the response I received from men and their advocates around the country. The book's stories and details of actual men gives voice to what men are feeling as they deal with gender discrimination.

Anecdotes are powerful stuff. I chose to use them because several male activists told me that the most successful way to change the political climate in the men's rights arena is to present stories that make men seem real. People relate to other people whom they view as human beings with feelings and reactions to injustices, not as facts and figures. Yes, those are important, too, and I included them in the book as well.

Here is the problem in working with issues of men's rights, though: Facts and figures often don't exist or are expressed through the views of biased academics or "experts" who have an agenda. That agenda might get them tenure with their feminist peers (both male and female) and lead to grants or prestige that will advance their career, or at least sell textbooks or get articles published in well-regarded journals. But it seldom leads to helpful, unbiased research on men and their problems.

I sympathize, though, with these researchers. What if you write the truth about what is happening to men and point out what you perceive to be injustices against them? You could lose respect and prestige and be treated with suspicion and hostility even if you are correct. If you don't believe me, look up the work of Murray A. Straus.[3] When he noted that, contrary to popular opinion, women play a large role in domestic violence, Straus received death threats. Why? Because he didn't fall in line with the academic sycophants. Forget about getting your work into journals or libraries. The gatekeepers will make sure that your voice is not heard. Readers, however, are not so easily dissuaded from learning the truth.

Men from around the country emailed, called on the phone, and wrote personal letters sent to both my office and my publisher to give me accounts of their own "strike" as well as feedback about the book. Their letters were personal, amazing, and at times heartbreaking and frustrating. For example, Joe wrote:

> When I was in the Marine Corps, I was sued by 11 different women for child support. When you are enlisted, much information about you becomes public record. Single mothers who are pressured by state welfare agencies to name a father find enlisted men who are stationed overseas and name them as the father.
>
> Now you're supposed to have 3 things to start a paternity claim, like you have to be in the same country as the mother at the time she gets pregnant, but no one cares about that. I got home from Afghanistan and found my bank account emptied out with no recourse . . . because I missed court hearings I didn't know were happening, and by default became the legal father of a child.

It's a huge scam, and no one cares. . . . The state gets their money back from a rube, and the mother stops getting hounded.[4]

The feedback and criticisms of the book were interesting, to say the least, and some of the criticism was warranted. Many readers felt that I did not include enough detail and wanted chapters expanded to explore more topics, such as men in the military who are taken advantage of by women and the courts (like Joe, above). Others suggested covering research of minority men and gay men's views on men's issues and presenting more on men's lack of reproductive rights, particularly those that are denied due to institutional bias.[5] The last point is crucial, especially regarding birth control for men. Shawn, a never-married fifty-five-year-old man from Massachusetts, noted:

In your discussion of men's lack of reproductive rights, you could have mentioned that some docs will not perform vasectomies on married men without written permission from their wives. They do it to protect themselves from lawsuits but still, try to imagine a woman needing written permission from her husband to get her tubes tied.[6]

I agree that this sexism (or fear of getting sued) on the part of doctors who perform vasectomies is important to mention. A woman would be outraged if her doctor suggested that her husband needed to give written approval for a tubal ligation. Men deal with this type of sexism all the time, and no one cares much. Sure, a few bloggers and websites take notice, and some do a good job of getting the issues out. But this should be an outrage, not a mention in a book or a few blogs. This reproductive sexism is unacceptable, and we should all speak up.

Katie Allison Granju, a mommy blogger, did just that as she wrote about the doctor who asked her permission when her husband went in for a vasectomy:

> But would it surprise you to learn that apparently, many doctors in this country REALLY DO require men who come to them seeking vasectomies to 'fess up to marital status, and to then get their wives' written consent before the physician will perform the procedure? In some cases, doctors require a face-to-face meeting with a man's wife—in addition to the signed consent from her—before a vasectomy will be performed.
>
> How did I discover this? Well, without getting all up in my husband's business by offering too many details, suffice it to say that he and I can now credibly report that this inexplicably retro violation of men's rights to privacy and medical autonomy actually *does* take place.[7]

The Good Men Project website followed up on Granju's discovery with a post wondering if spousal permission for a vasectomy was typical (or legal) and found that many doctors took matters into their own hands and imposed rules on a case-by-case basis:

> Well, according to Janet Crepps, a lawyer at the Center for Reproductive Rights, while there's absolutely no law requiring men to obtain their partner's consent, it *can* be imposed on a case-by-case basis at a clinical level.
>
> Doctors can impose requirements in a private setting in order to protect themselves legally. It's their choice that they want to do that. While it would be pretty difficult for a wife to successfully sue a doctor for doing a vasectomy on her husband, it wouldn't surprise me if their legal counsel insisted that they would be better off getting that consent. That said, nobody I know is imposing that kind of requirement.[8]

I have spoken to many men who said that a doctor refused to do a vasectomy without the wife's permission. This should never take place. Men are autonomous beings who have rights when it comes to reproduction.

Unfortunately, many sexist types feel that men don't deserve any reproductive rights and should simply keep their pants zipped. William Saletan at Slate.com had this to say in a recent article:

Here's the short version. First, for men: If you put your sperm anywhere near a woman's reproductive tract, you had better be prepared to raise a child with her. Your ejaculation is your signature on a contract authorizing her to carry any resulting pregnancy to term and to enlist you as the father. If you aren't prepared to sign that contract, ejaculate somewhere else. Don't complain later that you weren't consulted about subsequent decisions. The only decision you get is the one at the outset.[9]

This disturbing, rigid mindset is why so many men have gone on strike. In our society, men carry most of the responsibility with very little privilege. It may seem preferable at times to watch porn rather than to get near a woman, especially given the high stakes. As the technology for porn and sex improves, perhaps this will become a decent option. A better one would be to fight for fairer, saner laws and a more equitable society for men. I hope this paperback version of *Men on Strike* will contribute to that end.

In closing, I leave you with the words of a reader who took the time to mail me a letter about his own strike and how he felt about my book. Christian from Massachusetts wrote:

I felt such a release when reading it because someone out there finally has taken the time to explore and understand men and our unique experience of American society. Without realizing it, I think I've been on strike for years now. I know I've felt like "fair game" since I first saw Oprah on the airwaves in 1986. I was 16 at the time but it was clear that it was open season on males. As you demonstrate, that thinking has continued and become increasingly entrenched and accepted. . . . Your book made me feel appreciated, understood, and like I'm no longer walking alone.[10]

As a psychologist and an author, there is no greater reward for me than to hear that my book gave a reader hope, understanding, and a lessened sense of isolation. As noted above, men's rights may have a long way to go in our society given the rigid mindset against men. The good news is that there are many of us out there who are patient, unrelenting, and will not falter along the path to justice. I hope you are one of them.

Helen Smith, PhD
Knoxville, Tennessee

Prologue

Enslavement used to be based on race, now it's based on gender.
—Carnell Smith, advocate for male paternity fraud victims

If you are a wimp, this book is not for you. The suggestions I make in this book are difficult and require sacrifice and if you, as a male, do not feel you are up to the challenge, put this book down and go elsewhere. What I am going to describe to you requires a revolution to change the culture, and thus the political climate in this country that allows laws and actions against the male sex that would never be allowed against the female one.

Perhaps you think this is fair, that men should suffer for the ills of their ancestors and for the discrimination against women in the past. Maybe you are a chivalrous white-knight type who loves nothing more than the thought of saving a damsel in distress and would like to see your fellow man brought to his knees by laws that limit men's reproductive and personal lives as well as their livelihoods. Maybe you have political ambitions or work in a field that requires you to favor female privilege over male justice and you have no intention of changing because you benefit from this two-way arrangement. Maybe you are just a guy who wants to get laid and acts in a politically correct manner in the hope of getting more women. If so, you are not my audience, but you might want to stick around and learn something.

If you are a woman, the main focus of this book is on men but you may find some of the information of interest. It may help you to understand more about what the typical men are going through in this country and why they don't marry as readily anymore or go to college as often as they once did. Though you may disagree with much that is written here, keeping an open mind to how men *actually* feel and think as opposed to how the media, white knights and other women tell them how to think and feel may help you to understand how to connect with men in a more open and intimate way. Your husband, son, father or brother will thank you for it. And as Martin Luther King Jr. once said from a Birmingham jail, "injustice anywhere is a threat to justice everywhere." If we as women allow injustice to men today, who knows what will happen to us tomorrow? If learning about men rather than blaming them for all the ills of the world appeals to you, welcome.

My actual audience is the man who knows that something in today's twenty-first century is amiss. He can't put his finger on it exactly but feels deeply that modern society has turned its back on the average male. All around you, you hear the question, "Where have all the good men gone?" But you know instinctively that it's the wrong question. The right one is "Why have all the good men gone on strike?"

This book will tell you why and tell you and society how to fix it. Because if we don't, our society will never be the same. Our sons, brothers, fathers, uncles and husbands will live in a world where they will not know due process, where a man can be jailed for no other reason than that a woman pointed a finger at him, or because he raised his voice to her or where he can be placed into involuntary servitude to pay for eighteen years for a child that is not his. Oops! Too late. This is already happening in the United States of America.

Men are sensing the backlash against them and are consciously and unconsciously going "on strike." They are dropping out of college, out of the workforce, and out of marriage and fatherhood at alarming rates. So much so that a number of books have been written about this phenomenon in recent years that look at the "man-child" of today and summarize that he and his arrested development have taken a vacation from responsibility because he can, or because he can now get sex on demand.

Or worse, these books discuss how his irresponsible behavior has harmed females, since his only purpose on earth is to serve women. Nothing could be further from the truth. Most men are not acting irresponsibly because they are immature or because they want to harm women; they are acting *rationally* in response to the lack of incentives today's society offers them to be responsible fathers, husbands and providers. In addition, many are going on strike, either consciously or unconsciously, because they do not want to be harmed by the myriad of laws, attitudes and backlash against them for the simple crime of happening to be male in the twenty-first century. Men are starting to fight back against the backlash. This book explains their battle cry.

Introduction

Why is a woman writing this book? you ask. I thought the same thing for years. Let me tell you a bit about myself and give you some background on men's issues so that you will understand why I have come to the conclusion that there is a war against men in our culture that needs to be ended before it is too late. I will also tell you why, as a psychologist and as a woman, I am the person who should write this book.

I used to consider myself a feminist but mistakenly thought feminism meant equality between the sexes. In today's culture, it means female privilege, and I believe discrimination against men is every bit as bad as discrimination against women—and I want no part of it. Now men are the ones who are in need of justice and focus. I have been blogging and writing at my own blog, www.drhelen.blogspot.com, and working with PJ Media,[1] a libertarian and conservative online website and Internet TV media company, for some time, starting around 2005 for the former and 2007 for the latter. I now blog and write on men's issues and men's rights as a columnist and blogger for PJ Media exclusively as well as occasionally host an Internet TV show for PJTV focusing on men's issues.[2]

As you are probably well aware, men's issues are not exactly the topic du jour with the mainstream media outlets, unless you count the time I saw some poor guy being raked over the coals by Dr. Phil for daring to say that he did not feel he should have to pay child support for a baby that a woman tricked him into having by telling him that she had a medical condition and could not have children and was on birth control to boot. What nerve!

Anyway, my foray into writing about men's issues did not begin overnight. I have worked as a psychologist for over two decades and one of the first private clients I had was a wheelchair-bound man named John who was being beaten by his large and angry wife. My whole career took a different turn after that experience. I had known before that men didn't always get a fair shake, but with the evidence clearly in front of me and few resources to help a battered male, all I could do was try to help this guy get up the courage to get out of the situation.

I have spent many years talking to hundreds of men about their deepest, darkest secrets. Many have been afraid to talk and for others it was a relief, but the one thing they all had in common was a feeling that they were "wimps for having problems" and they felt a reluctance to go against what society expected of them: to provide for women and their families with nary a whimper. Even if the women were cheating on them, even if they were raising children alone and the women refused to help with support, and even if the children weren't theirs.

But the anger was there, seething below the surface, and in therapy it came forth in physical and emotional ways that wreaked havoc with these men and their bodies and minds. And they believed no one cared, because in reality, few did. Men kill themselves over pain like this and the statistics show they do it often. In 2010, the latest suicide statistics show that 38,364 people killed themselves nationally and 30,277 of those were men.[3]

How many of these men had decided to kill themselves because they could no longer see their children, had a broken relationship or were involved in a bitter divorce? Ironically, even when you look at the suicide statistics, mostly the concern seems to be about women who kill themselves. Apparently, our society cares so little about men that those who kill themselves are hardly news.

Even Thomas Ball, a man who set himself on fire on the courthouse steps because he felt jerked around by family court, was barely worth mentioning on the evening news for his dramatic ending. Ball, a fifty-eight-year-old New Hampshire man, stated that he was "done being bullied for being a man"[4] by the family court system. But despite his horrible and public death, his last act received little media attention. Just a few activists on the web and a few news outlets such as *International Business Times* and the *Keene Sentinel*, a paper in New Hampshire, picked it up. Men are literally killing themselves to get their concerns heard, but no one is listening.[5]

When no one listens, people tune out and start to do their own thing. There is a term for bailing out of the mainstream of society that I blogged about in 2008 called "Going John Galt"[6] or "going Galt" for short. Have you ever read *Atlas Shrugged*? If not, do so. If you have read the book, you know where I am going with this. In Ayn Rand's book, the basic theme is that John Galt and his allies take actions that include withdrawing their talents and "stopping the motor of the world" while leading the "strikers" (those who refused to be exploited) against the "looters" (the exploiters, backed by the government).[7] One interesting fact about *Atlas Shrugged* is that the original title was *The Strike*, but Rand changed it at her husband's suggestion.[8] The original title of Rand's book seems fitting for what is happening with today's twenty-first-century man.

In some sense, men today feel very much like Rand's characters in *Atlas Shrugged*, knowing that they can be exploited for their sense of duty, production and just for being male at any time. The state transfers men's production to women and children through child support, alimony, divorce laws, and government entitlements that are mainly for women, such as WIC (grants to states for women, infants and children) or welfare payments to single mothers. It is not only in family relationships that men are screwed, but also in many areas of modern society. Men are portrayed as the bad guys, ready to rape, pillage, beat or abuse women and children at the drop of a hat. From rape laws that protect women but not the men they may accuse falsely to the lack of due process in sexual harassment cases on college campuses to airlines that will not allow men (possible perverts!) to sit next to a child,[9] our society is at war with men and men know it full well.

In fact, men have known that a backlash against them has been happening for decades, so why is it taking so long for men to fight back? Psychologist Warren Farrell, in his prophetic book *The Myth of Male Power*, written in 1993, talks about "the men's movement as an evolutionary shift" and says the movement will be "the most incremental of movements" because it is "hard to confront the feelings we've learned to repress and hard to confront the women we've learned to protect."[10] Farrell believes that the greatest challenge of the men's movement will be "getting men to ask for help for *themselves*. Men were always able to ask for help on *behalf of others*— for a congregation, their wives, children, or a cause—*but not for themselves*."[11]

According to Farrell, "major movements have two core stimuli: 1) emotional rejection; and 2) *economic hurt*. **When a large number of people feel emotionally rejected and economically hurt at the same moment in history, a revolution is in the making.**"[12] Lord knows, men today are feeling emotionally rejected, not just if they divorce as Farrell discusses, but in many aspects of American life as I shall describe in the following chapters of this book. In addition, men are hurting economically, not just as husbands and fathers in a divorce, but also because of the current recession that has threatened men's livelihoods and long-term career prospects.

According to political scientist James Q. Wilson, "among the bottom fifth of income earners, many people, especially men, stay there their whole lives."[13] The economic and psychological ramifications that men are dealing with in today's society are the perfect storm of circumstances to propel men who have been on the sidelines to fight for their *own* justice, rather than for justice on behalf of others.

That's where this book comes in. If men have a psychological barrier to standing up for their own causes and in their personal relationships because of social conditioning and even evolution, then it is overcoming those barriers that will lead to legal and cultural changes for men that are equitable and fair. Of course, there are more than just psychological barriers to justice for men. There are legal barriers, but I truly believe that the culture drives politics and politics drives the law.

As a psychologist, I can teach you the tools to identify and overcome these barriers and, as a woman, I can share with you the information you need to deal with those women and men in your life whom you are afraid to confront on your way to equality. I will not apologize for being pro-male as so many authors and media types do. I find that disgusting. And face it, as a woman, I am not going to get as much grief as a man would for saying the same thing. I still get some, but the stakes aren't as high for me. But while my feelings matter somewhat, yours matter more in this fight. I can give you the tools, but much of the work will be up to you.

I once asked my husband what it took to be a "men's rights activist." "I'm not a man and I'm not brilliant," I told him, thinking these two traits would provide me with what I needed to work in that arena. My husband, a law professor and writer of a large political blog, stated, "You just need courage." That I have in spades, and, if you are reading this book, you probably do too. It's a good thing, because you will need this trait more than anything if you, your sons, your nephews, your brothers and fathers are to survive in today's feminized world of marriage, reproduction, college, public and private space and work. The following chapters will discuss these areas and the problems men are facing in each, and why so many of you, like the characters in *Atlas Shrugged*, have decided to go on strike.

MEN ON STRIKE

CHAPTER 1

The Marriage Strike

Why Men Don't Marry

I guess I'm one of the boycotters. . . . About 6 or 7 years ago I gradually just quit dating. Without really thinking about it, I came to the decision that I would not get married, so I wasn't interested in going through the hassle of dating. The interesting part is that I share a house with two other guys in similar situations. We all seem to have voluntarily removed ourselves not just from the population of marriageable men, but from the dating pool. One is a few years older than me, the other [is] in his early 30s. Both of them were previously married and don't seem eager to repeat the experience.

—A commenter named Ernie from PJMedia.com in response to my question, "Should Men Get Married?"[1]

There are many guys like Ernie all over the country who are no longer getting married. And why should they? Western culture has spent the past fifty years making marriage a better deal for women, while for men it's become a real ball and chain, sometimes almost literally. Men used to go to work, come home and, after a hard day's work providing for their families, they rested, ate dinner and felt like "the king of the castle." Fast forward to today, where the man works all day, comes home to cook or wash dishes, is chided for not doing a good enough job, is relegated to the basement while the wife and kids enjoy the run of the house, and spends the weekends watching the kids with a dirty diaper bag slung across his shoulders or hanging out in a shopping mall holding his wife's purse. On top of an already stressful life, he also gets a bunch of pitying stares from the younger men who wonder what he has become and how they can avoid the same fate.

Now, instead of equality in marriage, he can expect to share household tasks, act as unpaid bodyguard and home repairman, pay for most of the bills, help with the kids and, for all his efforts, be denigrated by the wife and society. And if he does fight back? He pays child support, gets half or more of his stuff taken and has to leave the house, and he might even get a restraining order or, worse, be charged with child or domestic abuse. What is there to gain?

It's no wonder that fewer and fewer men are getting married now than in the past. Kay Hymowitz states in her book, *Manning Up*, that "in 1970, 80 percent of 25- to 29-year-old men were married; in 2007, only about 40 percent of them were. In 1970, 85 percent of 30- to 34-year-old men were married; in 2007, only 60 percent of them were."[2]

Men no longer see marriage as being as important as they did even fifteen years ago. "According to Pew Research Center, the share of women ages eighteen to thirty-four that say having a successful marriage is one

of the most important things in their lives rose nine percentage points since 1997—from 28 percent to 37 percent. For men, the opposite occurred. The share voicing
this opinion dropped, from 35 percent to 29 percent."[3]

Even in middle age, fewer men are getting married,
especially those without a college degree. The *New York
Times* reports that "about 18 percent of men ages 40 to
44 with less than four years of college have never married, according to census estimates. That is up from
about 6 percent a quarter-century ago. Among similar
men ages 35 to 39, the portion jumped to 22 percent
from 8 percent in that time."[4] Even college-educated
men are marrying less often at 84 percent, which is a
decline of 9 percent since 1980.[5] And the marriage rates
in general keep plummeting. According to men's activists Glenn Sacks and Dianna Thompson:

> The US marriage rate has dipped 40% over the past
> four decades, to its lowest point ever. There are many
> plausible explanations for this trend, but one of the
> least mentioned is that American men, in the face
> of a family court system which is hopelessly stacked
> against them, have subconsciously launched a "mar-
> riage strike."[6]

There are many reasons that men are not marrying, and
one of them is certainly the marriage strike as described
by Sacks and Thompson. However, though family court

injustice plays a big part in why men are no longer marrying as often, it is just one aspect. Men have other psychological and legal concerns about marriage in today's post-feminist society that increase the likelihood of the marriage strike. This chapter will address those concerns and look to answer the question, "Why aren't men marrying as readily now as they did in the past?"

WHY MEN DON'T MARRY— FROM THE "EXPERTS'" PERSPECTIVE

As I read through all of the comments I have received from men around the country over the years on why they do not want to marry, I can't help but feel that many so-called experts are wrong when they say that men are poor communicators. My interactions and observations show that men often know their minds very well, but they are reluctant to communicate in interpersonal and political settings for fear of coming across as weak or, worse, being accused of being sexist or misogynistic. Or sometimes, they *are* communicating, it's just that no one is listening or people are actively rejecting what they say.

I have even had relatives or case workers—almost always women—who tell me that the boy or man they have accompanied for an evaluation or therapy will not talk; they are too closed down. Yet, not once in my twenty-plus-year career has one of those men or boys refused to talk. How did I get them to talk? I listened.

The problem today is that society is not listening to

what men have to say if they do open up, and, at the same time, the risks for men in talking about these politically charged issues keep them silent, making it hard to glean the truth. Even those experts or authors who write books on the topic of male reluctance to marry and who profess to be somewhat pro-male seem to get it wrong. What they don't realize is that the incentives to marry have changed for men, and they are no longer willing to risk so much more than in previous years to gain potentially so much less.

Authors Kay Hymowitz and Kathleen Parker have written books that, on the surface, seem to advocate for men. Hymowitz's *Manning Up: How the Rise of Women Has Turned Men into Boys*[7] and Kathleen Parker's *Save the Males: Why Men Matter, Why Women Should Care*[8] are a good start to recognizing the war against men in our society, but the condescending titles alone give the impression that the authors care not so much about men as about how men relate to women. This is not to say these two books aren't important. They are, as they give some good background on how and why society treats men in unhealthy ways. But I do have some serious criticisms.

Newsflash: If you want to be pro-male, using terms like "child-man in the promised land," as Hymowitz does, is not the way to do it—and, frankly, comparing "saving the males" to "saving the whales" as Parker's book does is, well, insulting. It implies that men are comparable to animals, which of course is how some women and their sexist male counterparts think.

When reading through these two books, I get the impression not that men are autonomous beings who deserve equality as equal citizens in a democratic society, but rather that they should be treated well enough so that they will want to marry women, have children and support them so that *women* will have a better life. I have a different take: I propose that men are autonomous beings who are entitled to justice and equality and the pursuit of their *own* happiness because they are human beings in a supposedly free society. Too bad this is such a radical departure that a whole book has to be written just to make this point. One would think it would be obvious, but it is not obvious in today's America.

Other books, such as *Guyland*[9] by Michael Kimmel or *Boys Adrift: The Five Factors Driving the Growing Epidemic of Unmotivated Boys and Underachieving Young Men*[10] by Leonard Sax, along with Hymowitz's book, treat the men's lack of interest in marriage as a kind of extended adolescence where men sit around playing video games and farting in order to ward off having to grow up. And all these "guys are losers" types stick together to add fuel to the negative image of men as boys. For example, Richard Whitmire, the author of *Why Boys Fail*[11]—another positive title!—endorses Hymowitz's book by stating:

Kay Hymowitz does an exacting job describing the growing flock of man/children we're seeing, and she lays out the disturbing reality of the "marriageable mate" dilemma. . . . Not only are there fewer college-educated men to marry, but many of those men who are available are little more than man/children—not anyone you would want your daughters to marry![12]

As if that endorsement of Hymowitz's book isn't bad enough as an example of the condescension these men's issues writers have for their subjects, Hymowitz, who professes herself to be "sympathetic" to men,[13] has a chapter called "Child-Man in the Promised Land." This chapter pokes fun at the men of today who refuse to grow up and who also—much to her chagrin—refuse to participate in "more civilized society":

Nothing attests to the SYM's [straight young male's] growing economic and cultural muscle more than video games. Once upon a time, video games were for little boys. . . .

Indeed, the child-man's home sweet media home is the Internet, where no meddling censor or nervous advertiser can come between him and his desires. . . . Contemporary undomesticated SY maledom appears in its darkest form in the person of Tucker Max, whose eponymous website is a favorite among his peers. . . . Crudity is at the heart of the child-man persona—the bad-boy tone epitomizes his refusal to grow up—but Max remains fixated on his penis and his "dumps" like a toddler stuck somewhere around the oedipal stage.[14]

Another of these books on the decline of men is Hanna Rosin's *The End of Men and the Rise of Women*, which is frankly the most matronizing of all of these books.[15] Rosin's main thesis is that women have pulled ahead of men in many areas of society and are able to adapt and be flexible at home and work in ways that men cannot. In fact, in her book she refers to the "Plastic Woman" who is able to bend and do everything at once and who is climbing the ladder past men. These loser men are referred to as "Cardboard Men," who are apparently inflexible and unable to adapt to the new world order.

What she doesn't mention is that this new world order is a place where men are discriminated against, forced into a hostile environment in school and later in college, and held in contempt by society—and for the honor, are expected to conform to a society for women only. What she calls inflexibility is men rejecting her and other feminists' suggestions that they become more like women. She has no clue how men really feel or why they behave the way they do, nor does she seem to care.

Case in point: Even her young son is appalled at the title of her book. In an interview with *The Daily Beast*, we learn the following:

> There are a few things that happen when you attempt to travel the streets of New York with a bright yellow book that screams *The End of Men* under your arm.

First, you get a lot of inquisitive stares. Some people snicker. When you accidentally leave the book on the counter of your morning coffee shop, the man who returns it to you points to the cover, giggles, and does a little jig.

But if you are the author of a book called *The End of Men*—with a man for a husband and a boy for a child—you get sticky notes left on your bedroom door. "My 6-year-old, to whom the book is dedicated, writes things like, 'Only *bullies* write books called *The End of Men*,'" says author Hanna Rosin, whose 2010 Atlantic essay turned 310-page book hit stands this week. She clarifies: "He's learning about bullying in school."[16]

It seems that Rosin's young son, Jacob, has a better grasp of gender relations than this "celebrated" feminist who doesn't have a clue. Yes, Jacob, mommy is a bully, and maybe when you grow up, you will lead the revolution that teaches bullies like your mom that men are not defective girls.

How are men going to grow up and relate well to women if women don't seem to like them?

Clowns, failures, unmotivated and child-men: With friends like the authors mentioned, who needs enemies? Publishers and women complain that men don't read self-help or relationship books, but after reading these books, who can blame them? How many women would buy books where women were made out to be failure-to-launch goofballs who couldn't carry their own weight? I do think that some of these books have merit and are at least attempting to shed light on male development, and a couple of these books even include interviews with actual men. However, they do so in a way that is unflattering to men to say the least and they reinterpret men's behavior to give credence to their views of men as uncivilized, verbally stunted semibarbarians who refuse to do what society expects of them: Marry women and shut the hell up!

These books treat men and their behavior as the problem, but that's superficial. The real question is: *What is it about our society that has made growing up seem so unattractive to these men?*

Maybe there is no incentive to grow up anymore. It used to be that being a grown-up, responsible man was rewarded with respect, power and deference. Now you get much less of that, if any at all. You have spent much of your youth confronted with "Boys Are Stupid" T-shirts, listened in health class as you are told you are a potential rapist, had your girlfriend talk about "cutting off your balls" without a thought and, of course, there were no repercussions. By college, you realize that the hostility is coming at you like a knife.

And as you get older, it only gets worse, and the younger guys know it. As a post-college man, you are now seen by the media as a buffoon, a potential pervert, a bumbling dad—if not a deadbeat—and your wife gives you a death stare if you don't satisfy her every whim.[17] You might even have a child and find out later that it's not yours, yet you still have to pay up. In short, you are a sucker if you grow up and fulfill what society now expects of the average married male. You have few rights and even less dignity. And what about the perks if you don't get married and grow up? It turns out that there are many, as I discovered with a little digging.

First off, if you live with your girlfriend, research shows you *might* be happier than if you got married. A *Men's Health* article mentioned one such study that followed 2,737 people for six years and found that cohabiters said they were happier and more confident than married couples and singles.[18] Live-in girlfriends even stay thinner on average than wives.[19] There are many reasons that those living together are happier than married couples, such as "cohabiters tend to have fewer expectations on each other, nixing unwanted obligations."[20]

This means that men who live with girlfriends rather than get married may not be taken for granted as often, as it seems that married women often treat their husbands more like the hired help than an equal partner. Men who are married tend to see their friends and family less often, which can harm their self-esteem.[21] Marriage is also more likely to end in financial risk for a man if he is divorced. And just as important, the psychological risks for men in marriage are greater than they were in the past. Women are told constantly by society that they are "empowered" and this often translates into a man working, earning a living, helping with the housework and being relegated to the basement while the rest of the family enjoys the entire house. Does he get rewarded for this behavior? No, he is often second to his wife, the kids and even the dog. Hence, all the "doghouse" references that reinforce the idea that if he doesn't buck up and do what society and the wife expect of him, punishment will follow.[22] Though it seems funny, it's not. Society has stacked the deck against men in modern marriage, and the guys know it.

Ultimately, society is asking men to do something that is going against their own interests. Their lives as single men are fulfilling, happy and, if not respected, at least envied by their married brethren. Life as a married man is often difficult with few perks and little in the way of respect or rights. The discrepancy between the life of the freer, single man and the life of the less respected, less free life of the married man is at the heart of why so many men have gone on strike. This discrepancy between the perks of single life and the punishment of married life for men has become wider in modern times given the unequal legal terms, cultural empowerment for married women—but not men—and the lack of reproductive rights that men face in comparison to their female counterparts.

WHY MEN DON'T MARRY—
FROM THE MAN'S PERSPECTIVE

As I sifted through these men-are-losers with-a-twist books, I found that a major flaw with many of them is that they lack a man's perspective—even if they were written by a man. They theorize about why men don't want to marry or they look at stereotypical books and magazines such as *Maxim* that make guys out to be horndogs—nothing wrong with that, but men are more than their sexual urges—as a lens to evaluate men's lack of enthusiasm for whisking a woman away in matrimonial bliss. But using *Maxim* and guys like hook-up artist Tucker Max—or even digging up hard-partying frat guys as examples of normal men and their feelings about marriage—is like using *Sex in the City, Cosmo* or sorority girls to describe all women's views of relationships. It's rather narrow.

And even if researchers do interview men, the media, journalists or the researchers themselves often apply negative interpretations to the reasons that men do not want to grow up and get married. They still seem to think that marriage and the concept of being grown-up has something to offer men. But when you look at the behavior and misinterpret the reasons behind it, the truth still remains elusive. They treat men more like resources that haven't been extracted yet, rather than human beings who make rational decisions.

For example, I found some research done by researchers at Rutgers University that looked like a decent study on why men don't get married, until I looked a little closer. Sixty "not-yet-married" men were interviewed in northern New Jersey, Chicago, Washington, D.C., and Houston. The men were ages twenty-five to thirty-three, and none of them was gay. The researchers found that the top three reasons that men did not marry was "they can get sex without marriage more easily than in times past," "they can enjoy the benefits of having a wife by cohabiting rather than marrying," and "they want to avoid divorce and its financial risks."[23]

The interpretation? Men don't need to get married to get what they want these days—mainly sex. But dig a little deeper and you find this statement in the article: "Men see marriage as a final step in a prolonged process of growing up." One of the Rutgers' researchers, David Popenoe, in a *New York Times* piece on marriage, says "men do not marry because they do not want to. As unwilling to commit as ever, men have been let off the hook by more permissive social mores that have made it acceptable to live together and raise children out of wedlock."[24]

Yes, perhaps men do feel less pressure to marry, which is a good thing in many ways. But rather than "let off the hook by permissive social mores,"[25] the real reason many rational men do not marry is that the incentives have changed and growing up is no longer a reward but a punishment for men—so why do it? More readily available sex may be the by-product of not having to grow up, but to grow up to possibly *not* get sex, to lose your dignity, your rights, your kids, and possibly your financial freedom *and* to be hurt is hardly worth the chance for some, and can be suicidal for others. Instead of spending our time trying to figure out how to get men to commit to marriage in its current state, we should be asking more questions like *how can we make marriage more appealing to young men so that they want to get married?* And why have so many men gone on a marriage strike?

Why not talk to some normal, everyday guys and the people who work with them to shed light on these questions? First, we must understand what normal, everyday guys in their natural habitats think of marriage and do so without the preconceived notion that they are losers who are failing to launch if they won't satisfy a woman's every whim. What a novel idea! "Where are these odd birds?" I wondered. Since many men seem to go underground these days, I decided to check around to see if I could find some of the haunts that these guys frequent. I figured that guys like technology, so a good place to start would be on the Internet and in the gaming world of guys who like video games. One good thing about the Internet: People are more likely to say in cyberspace what they will not say to your face. After all, studies consistently show that people tend to reveal more personal and potentially embarrassing information in a computer-administered interview than a face-to-face interaction.[26]

WHAT MEN ON THE INTERNET
ARE SAYING ABOUT MARRIAGE

It is said that men can't handle intimacy. That's not it at all.
It is sadness that men can't handle and they fear that intimacy
will take them there.
—Jack at *Dr. Helen* blog [27]

Since I have a men's rights blog, I looked back at some
posts on marriage where I had asked men if they wanted
to marry and, if not, why? I initially made the mistake
of suggesting that men who didn't marry were missing
out. [28] My readers set me straight about the ramifications
of being married in a society that puts women's legal
and psychological needs first and men's needs last or not
at all. First off, let me say that I am a libertarian and do
not believe much in the state being involved in marriage
in the first place. I think people should have the right to
decide for themselves the rules of their marriages and
should do so with private contracts. However, since the
state *is* involved and I don't make the rules, let's deal
with the real world.

I followed up the marriage blog post with an article
for PJ Media that asked men if they should marry, and
hundreds of readers contributed their experiences; many
did so anonymously. [29] There was a lot of anger and sadness in the responses and typically, you know what that
means to the politically correct or even the white-knight
crowd: Men who complain are either wimps or misogy-

nists or both. In reality, they are usually neither. Plenty of feminists are angry or sad, after all, but those emotions are just seen as lending authenticity to their complaints. The men who responded to the question I posed had legitimate legal and psychological concerns. Some of the commenters felt that marriage was too much of a risk for men and had been warned by other men not to make a mistake. Here is one example from an anonymous commenter:

> Problem is, at least 7 out of 10 guys I talk to tell me that it is one of the worst mistakes that they ever made. Some tell me not to marry American women, that they are all feminist at heart. One married guy told me that I could get the same effect by selling my house, giving all my money away and having someone castrate me. This is really starting to unnerve me and the more I learn about the legal bias against men, I'm beginning to back off of marriage. I love my girlfriend, but all of these guys say their girlfriends changed once they married and begin to dominate and control. I am starting to think marriage in America cannot be saved.[30]

Still others, such as the following commenter, have made commitments to marriage but found out they were on the short end of the stick from both the women and the law once they were in the middle of a divorce:

I met a woman that I was sure was my soul mate. I was deeply in love and so, I thought, was she. All this changed when I lost my high paying job through downsizing. To my credit, I went to work immediately and had two jobs, but still only made about 80% of my old income. My wife gave me a year and then began sleeping with a man, who hadn't lost his job, in my bed while I was at work. She left with him, taking almost all of my savings and anything else she could carry. Her explanation was that she was "an expensive bitch" and she was unhappy because I worked so much. The adultery doesn't seem to matter to the court and she got essentially everything. Besides the financial losses, I was so devastated by the betrayal that I could barely function for months. She treated me like garbage and I never worked harder at any endeavor in my life.[31]

Another commenter by the name of "confused" stated:

… the problem is that marriage is quite explicitly NOT a contract in our modern society. Instead, it's a collection of whatever the judiciary/legislature decides it is today.[32]

Psychologically astute commenter Jack weighed in with:

It is said that men can't handle intimacy. That's not it at all. It is sadness that men can't handle and they fear that intimacy will take them there.[33]

Barry states:

> Personally I hate the idea that a woman can stop anything and everything I care about doing just by making my life a living hell until I concede to her demands. I must hold my tongue, hold my temper and "be the man there" while the spouse screams invectives and shouts how I should stop riding my bike, horse etc. if I loved her! And let's not even go to the "I want you to stop riding the bike, horses etc. because YOU WANT TO," not because I am bitching you off of the bike, horse etc. You name the hobby and the only recourse is divorce where the state takes all my toys and gives them to her. Yes, marriage ain't what it used to be.[34]

Though some will dismiss these men's voices as bitter rants on the Internet, in hearing the more angry or frustrated views of those who speak out, we can understand better what many other men secretly think but won't say. In doing so, we can learn what truly needs to be changed for men to feel that marriage is a more rewarding experience. Next, let's turn to what guys who like video games think of women and marriage.

WHAT GAMERS ARE SAYING ABOUT MARRIAGE

A lot of the guys who opt out aren't particularly angry at women, they just don't see much point to pursuing involvement with them.
—Vox Day, game designer and blogger at *Alpha Game* blog

Source: http://alphagameplan.blogspot.com/2012/02/introducing-hypergamouse.html

Vox Day is a blogger who runs the *Alpha Game* blog that is summed up with the following caption across the top: "Breaking the chains, winning the games, and saving Western Civilization."[35] He is also a game designer and author who is interested in the plight of the modern male. His site is a place for guys to discuss the difficulties of modern relationships, video games and just general guy stuff. Although not all of the men who go on the site are gamers—those who play video games—a number of them are, and it's a good place to gather information on how gamers think in terms of marriage.

Before I turn to the marriage information, let's learn a few important terms that will help add perspective to the data. Much of the conversation on the *Alpha Game* blog and many others that are interested in "pickup-artist theory"[36] is about hypergamy, which is a term used for females' tendency to want to "marry up." James Taranto, in a *Wall Street Journal* article on American women, says that hypergamy "more broadly defined as the female tendency to mate with dominant or high-status males or to be selective about one's choice of mate—is also widely observed in other species."[37]

Vox Day, like so many of the pickup artist bloggers, has a male socio-sexual hierarchy that he uses to classify men. Here are a few of his classifications and their characteristics:

Alphas—the male elite, the leaders of men for whom women naturally lust.

Betas—the lieutenants, the petty aristocracy. They're popular, they do well with women, they're pretty successful in life, and they may even be exceptionally good-looking. But they lack the Alpha's natural self-confidence and strength of character.

Deltas—the normal guys. Deltas are the great majority of men. They can't attract the most attractive women, so they usually aim for the second-tier women with very limited success, and stubbornly resist paying attention to all of the third-tier women who are comfortably in their league. This is ironic, because Deltas would almost always be happier with their closest female equivalents. When a Delta does manage to land a second-tier woman, he is constantly afraid that she will lose interest in him and will, not infrequently, drive her into the very loss of interest he fears by his non-stop dancing of attendance upon her. In a social setting, the Deltas are the men clustered together in groups, each of them making an occasional foray towards various small gaggles of women before beating a hasty retreat when direct eye contact and engaged responses are not forthcoming. Deltas tend to put the female sex on pedestals and have overly optimistic expectations of them; if a man rhapsodizes about his better half or is an inveterate White Knight, he is almost certainly a Delta. Deltas like women, but find them mysterious, confusing, and are sometimes secretly a little afraid of them.

Gammas—the obsequious ones, the posterior puckerers, the nice guys who attempt to score through white-knighting, faux-chivalry, flattery, and omnipresence. All men except true Alphas will occasionally fall into Gamma behavior from time to time . . .

Sigmas—the lone wolves. Occasionally mistaken for Alphas, particularly by women and Alphas, they are not leaders and will actively resist the attempt of others to draft them. Alphas instinctively view them as challenges and either dislike or warily respect them.

Omegas—the losers. Even the Gamma males despise them. That which doesn't kill them can make them stronger, but most never surmount the desperate need to belong caused by their social rejection. Omegas can be the most dangerous of men because the pain of their constant rejection renders the suffering of others completely meaningless in their eyes.[38]

Hypergamy and the classifications are important to understand as we look at the world of gamers and men who are not the alphas of the male world: Think of *The Big Bang Theory* characters who would be seen as Gammas or Omegas, who are are the men on the lower end of the dating pool. Do the least and most desirable men avoid marriage? Let's see.

Vox Day put up a request on his site for readers to reveal their demographic information and gathered general information about their marital status, desire for marriage and their self-perceived classification such as Alpha, Beta and so on. Here is what he found:

There were 141 male responses and 14 female responses. In order to more meaningfully calculate the income and partner averages, I threw out the top five and bottom five male outliers and the top and bottom female outliers.

First, the men. Their average age is 37.8 years (median 37) with an average annual income of $74.8 ([median is] $65k) and 7 ([median is] 3) lifetime sexual partners. 76% are religious, 24% are not. 49% are married, 51% are unmarried, and 14% have been divorced. Most of the divorced men remain unmarried.

The 80/20 rule is largely substantiated. Even if the outliers aren't included, the 20% (27) most sexually successful men had sex with 617 of the 921 women involved, or 67% of them. But since the Alphas and Sigmas by definition, [are] outliers, it's necessary to include them here even though we didn't in attempting to determine what is average. Including all 10 outliers meant that the 28 most sexually successful men had sex with 1099 of the 1447 women, or 76%. So, in the interest of precision, it should probably henceforth be described as the 75/20 rule, wherein 20 percent of the men are having 75% of the sexual encounters.

Women were significantly more pro-marriage than men. 86% of women were either satisfied with their marriage or interested in getting married versus 63% of men. In general, divorced and irreligious men were the most likely to be anti-marriage. Younger men were very slightly less likely to be pro-marriage, but the average difference between the pro- and anti-marriage camps was only one year. To the extent that the "marriage strike" exists, it appears to cover the full range of male ages.

Monetary success does tend to correlate with sexual success for men. The average income of the 28 ALPHAs, who had an average age of 38, was 50% higher than the average at $112k. The average income of the male virgins, whose average age was 31, was 16%

lower than the norm at $63k. Now, obviously the additional seven years was an advantage in providing more time to increase income and gain sexual experience, though not enough to account for the full disparity. And yet, money is clearly not the only determinant since there are ALPHAs with no income and virgins with very high incomes. Still, throwing out just one outlier on both ends would make the correlation even stronger.

There is a noticeable difference between the Alphas and the High Alpha players. The obvious dividing line there is around 40+ partners. So, there is the all-important distinction many women have requested. Any man with more than 30+ historical partners should probably be assumed to be a ruthless player intrinsically unfit for a long-term relationship as 62% of the men in this category were anti-marriage. Only the male virgins, at 66%, were more strongly anti-marriage. Compare to this the 80% of Alphas in the 15–30 partner category who were pro-marriage; all of those in this category who were anti-marriage were irreligious and most were divorced.[39]

So what does all of this mean as far as sex, marriage and gamers are concerned? Some interesting tidbits arise. It seems that men who have had more than thirty partners are less interested in marriage, as are men who are virgins, who are the most anti-marriage. The High Alpha men with numerous partners might be players and just enjoy being that way. But, female readers, take note: Those Alpha men with fifteen to thirty partners are the *most* marriage-minded. Perhaps if an Alpha is not an all-out player, he is more likely to have the confidence and prior positive experience to believe he can make a marriage work and is confident enough to feel that nothing will go wrong legally or otherwise.

However, the non-Alphas tell a different story. For those men who are not Alphas, many fewer women are available. If 24 percent of the men are sharing 76 percent of the women, the sexual prospects are poor for the 76 percent of men who are sharing the other 24 percent of women. Perhaps of those 76 percent, some are the virgins who are the most anti-marriage or are less marriage-minded because they have fewer women to choose from or feel socially rejected. It would be interesting to see if the men who are more in the Beta and lower classifications are playing more video games. Vox Day had this to say about the younger gamers with whom he has had contact:

I probably have a unique perspective on it due to my connections to the young guys in the gaming industry. It's bizarre how some of them are in their twenties, have graduated from good schools, and have simply zero interest in women. They just have literally nothing in common with them and no interest in them.

The "strike" theory is generally correct, I think. The problem is that games and porn are entertaining, inexpensive, easily accessible, and reliable. Women can be entertaining, but they're expensive, inaccessible for most men, and from the male perspective, shockingly unreliable. I would say that porn has raised the bar somewhat—it's bound to be seriously annoying when Little Miss Real Life won't give head when Jane Pornstar is twice as hot and is cheerfully performing all sorts of acrobatic stunts. And if you think about it, is a real woman who is average and only wants to have missionary-style sex once a week, minus a week for her period, actually any better than a wide variety of gorgeous porn stars catering to every bizarre fetish the Japanese can imagine and available on demand? It's not quite so clear once you put it in those terms. The biggest communication problem is that most women see "relationship" as a positive thing. Most men see it as an ambiguous thing. So, when the selling point of Little Miss Real Life over Jane Pornstar is "relationship," you can see where it's not going to be very appealing. I don't think there's much of a "fuck you" element, though. The guys who think that way tend to be the players, particularly the Sigma players. A lot of the guys who opt out aren't particularly angry at women, they just don't see much point to pursuing involvement with them.[40]

Are video games that good, or are they giving those 76 percent of men who have to share 24 percent of the women a place to go where they feel good, masculine and alive, and where they feel more like an Alpha? Or as James Taranto of the *Wall Street Journal* said about guys who prefer video games to girls: "there's a reason they're attracted to that particular pursuit. Video games are a simulacrum of masculine virtue: challenge, mastery, control."[41] The Alpha question? That will have to be a question for future research. Meanwhile, let's toss in some real-life guys who can shed more light on the marriage question.

WHAT MEN IN THE GYM AND AT THE BAR ARE SAYING ABOUT MARRIAGE

> *Eight out of ten girls my age today are "sketchy."*
> —Twenty-three-year-old Max at the gym on
>   why men don't want to get married early

> *Marriage is a dying concept.*
> —Twenty-four-year-old Jamie, when asked
>   why men don't get married as often

I continued my search for everyday men out and about in the world and decided that the local gym might be a good place to informally target men who might be willing to talk about their views on marriage. I had been watching young and middle-aged men at a local gym for weeks and sizing up a few as potential interviewees. As I stared and watched many of them working out with weights, I caught their eyes and was a bit afraid that they thought I was a cougar on the prowl for some fresh prey. If only they knew it wasn't that exciting. I was just there trying to find some potential research victims.

I finally approached a guy named "Max" who agreed to participate when I explained my book and need for his input. He seemed a bit reluctant at first, but when I told him that his interview would be anonymous and his name would be changed, he agreed. I could tell that he wasn't sure if he should say anything negative and searched my face for a reaction. When he saw that I wasn't upset or angered by anything that he said, he seemed to speak more openly about how men feel about marriage and women.

Max was a thoughtful twenty-three-year-old, muscular, white college student with blond hair from Michigan who told me up front that he had a girlfriend. "Do you want to get married?" I asked, to which he replied, "yes," but admitted he was one of the "lucky" ones. When I asked him why, he stated that his girlfriend was trustworthy and honest, kind of like himself. He had been dating her for about a year and things had been going well.

He was raised by a single mother and his father left when he was young. His stepfather came into the home and acted as his dad, and his mother became a very happy person. "It was so much better with my stepfather there. My mother wasn't lonely anymore. One of my uncles is divorced and I see how alone and lonely he is. My sister is also divorced, so yeah, I think about how marriage might not work out." Max seemed a bit naive when it came to the legalities of marriage, stating that he had taken some classes in college on law but he didn't know much about family court. He assumed that if he got divorced because his wife had cheated on him or done something wrong, the courts would be fair and lean in his favor. He did acknowledge, however, that "our society has shifted towards women. Even my stepdad makes all the money and my mother makes all the choices."

Max didn't seem quite as naive when it came to choosing women. "Most of my friends won't even consider marriage until their late twenties. A couple of them have been in love and got hurt when they were younger and I think that's why they don't want to get married now. I think girls a long time ago, maybe forty or fifty years ago, were doing less cheating and were more trustworthy. Now girls are more like guys used to be. I would say that eight out of ten girls now are 'sketchy' and about six or seven guys out of ten are those that girls can trust."

When I questioned him as to what "sketchy" meant, he replied that "a lot of girls today are crazy partiers; they flirt with other people and have sex with other guys. If they sleep with you on the first date, they are more likely to go off with someone else while they are with you. I think that's why guys are waiting to get married; they have to go through eight of the ten girls to find the two that aren't sketchy."

I asked Max if it was available sex that made it more attractive to stay single, but his feeling seemed to be that readily available sex wasn't necessarily the reason that guys didn't want to marry. He explained that readily available sex, though, was a marker of a possibly untrustworthy woman; if she slept with you on the first date, she might sleep with your buddy on the next one. "My girlfriend made me wait," he stated. He also added that as an accounting major, he did a cost-benefit analysis of marriage and felt that, for him, the benefits outweighed the costs. He does think he is unusual in his desire for marriage, as many of his friends have no interest.

In the past, having a sketchy wife who cheated was frowned upon and there were repercussions to her for doing so. Now cheating women are celebrated and encouraged by the culture. Even Whoopi Goldberg nonchalantly talked about how she cheated on her husband with little judgment or repercussions by society. In an interview, she stated, "is screwing around five or six times while married and with different men for that matter something you can say casually? In the celebrity world perhaps."[42] But if you are Tiger Woods, you can be hit in the head with a golf club if you cheat and society cheers on your wife for being empowered. You will also lose much of your income and assets in divorce court and may even lose your kids, even if the wife cheats. And you are always cast as the bad guy: People wonder what *you* did to make your wife cheat. If a man cheats, on the other hand, the wife is a victim and he's a louse who deserves punishment.

Now that the risk in marriage for men is so high,

guys must be much more careful about whom they marry. Neither the law nor the culture will support them if they make the wrong choice. Women are the empowered sex and their sexuality is celebrated. Men's sexuality is much more controlled by the legal system and society, even—or maybe especially—in marriage.

My next interviewee at the gym was Jamie, a twenty-four-year-old who sells gym memberships and works fifty to sixty hours a week. He grew up in Oak Ridge, Tennessee, and told me that his parents had been married twenty-seven years. "I don't plan to get married until I am around thirty and I can afford it." Jamie went to community college and has an associate's degree in business administration. He would like to go on to a four-year college but said that he heard there was a high drop-out rate at the local state college and he didn't know if it would be worth it.

He is living with two other male friends who are around his age and he pays his own way. He has a girlfriend and said that they go out on weekend nights when he has time, but he likes to sleep and cook when he is at home and doesn't have a lot of time. "For most of my friends, marriage is the furthest thing from their mind," he stated, and explained, "My generation spends a lot of time partying and there really isn't much loyalty. If you are out and meet a girl or a girl you are seeing meets a guy, you might be interested in that person. You might hook up." Jamie felt that his generation was influenced by celebrities and reality TV where everyone is partying and having a good time. "You see Kanye West and he has all these girls, not just one." He does have a married friend "who can't go out much because he has to stay home more often." Jamie described marriage as a "dying concept" because people just seem to hook up, have kids and move on. He said that not getting married made a person "a lot more free."

Jamie seemed to have a sense of learned helplessness in regards to a man's part in sex, marriage or reproduction. He told me about a friend who, when he was twenty or so, was partying with a seventeen-year-old girl. The friend is unable to get a job now because the girl's parents pressed charges and he is on a sex-offender registry. When asked how he would feel if this happened to him, Jamie just shrugged and said, "If the government passes strict laws, there's nothing I can do. I can just make a choice not to do that." I pointed out that he may not have a choice; for example, if he was in college and a girl said that he had sexually assaulted her, he might be found guilty by the school without a preponderance of evidence, even if he were innocent.

His reply? "Because of TV and the culture, the society would just believe that the girl was a victim and the guy was guilty." Jamie's way of handling his lack of rights as a male was to hope that nothing happened to him and if it did, to just react at that time. His one visible sign of anger came when we were discussing paternity issues and he said that he would "go to jail" rather than pay for a child that was not his. It didn't seem to occur to him that fighting for just laws was even an option. I wondered if his lack of interest in marriage was just an unconscious way of lessening the chance that he would be involved in a potentially difficult and helpless situation. He had told me he learned in school that if something was potentially dangerous, like drugs or hanging out with much younger girls, it was best to avoid it. Maybe his lack of interest in marriage has as much to do with avoiding a risky situation in order to "stay free" as it does with partying and having a good time, though the latter is certainly a reason for him.

What about older guys? Are they savvier than the younger guys about marriage and its potential risk? It seems so, at least with my next interviewees. I figured another good place to meet guys would be at a bar, thinking that if guys had been drinking, they might be more willing to open up. As the saying goes, *in vino veritas*—a Latin phrase that translates to "in wine [there is the] truth." Here is an example of a couple of the guys I met. I was introduced to John at an open bar at a reception in Washington, D.C., and when he heard that I was writing a book on men's views and attitudes about marriage, he seemed happy to open up.

John is a Jewish lawyer who is around fifty years old and has been divorced for more than twelve years. He said that after his daughter was born, his wife "went crazy" and they were divorced. I didn't get into any details, but it sounded somewhat like postpartum depression, though it must have been pretty bad since the marriage ended over it. John has dated throughout the past twelve years, and when I asked why he had never married again, he said he had not found anyone whom he was head over heels in love with. I asked about what types of women he liked to date, and he said, "I'm sure you will judge me if I tell you."

"Try me," I said, and he sheepishly stated that he was only attracted to women between the ages of twenty-five to thirty-five. I thought it was going to be something more risqué than an attraction to younger women that is so common for older men. I wondered why he thought it was unusual. He's probably just gotten an earful from women in the past who were upset about his preferences if they were past his prime age group. It's pretty much evolutionary for men to like younger women. I shrugged, and he continued.

John added that he understood, as a man and as a lawyer, that it was very risky these days for men to marry because the law does not favor men and they have to be more careful when looking for a committed relationship. "Marriage is an option that has some appeal, although remarriage in my case carries a more elevated set of risks than I considered when I was younger. The law tilts strongly against men in divorce; this does not affect dating so much but makes me gun shy about women who appear tough or cynical or hint at any anger or litigious issues." I asked him why twenty-five- to thirty-five-year-old women were more attractive to him, but rather than just the typical reasons you'd expect—

such as that they're more attractive, look up to me, and so on—he stated, "women in their mid thirties or so may be anxious for a family, and therefore I cannot always be sure they do not see me as a sperm donor or meal ticket, at least as the relationship begins." He said he would not mind having a baby, but he did not want that to be the primary reason a woman wanted to marry him, and that he truly wanted to find someone he was crazy about and who was crazy about him.

While it may just seem that John is another middle-aged guy in search of a younger hottie, it goes deeper than that. He is afraid he will be used by a woman exclusively for children and a possible meal ticket. While this is always a concern for many men, if a woman is forty years old and wants kids, it is even more of a concern. In the past, women had already had children by their late thirties or by forty, but now there are many who, because of technology, birth control and longer life spans, are older and who are looking for men to have a child or children. And the risks of remarriage are higher than they were in the past; men have more to lose in a divorce, and, with additional children, the stakes go up. Does she love him, his money, or his sperm? Men aren't so sure, and the courts and legal system make it even more difficult.

I met another older guy in Washington, D.C., who worked as a bartender at a popular restaurant in the middle of Georgetown. Bruce is fifty years old, and I ran into him while he was working one night and I was eating in his restaurant. To my surprise, he had read my blog and was eager to talk about his single status. "I've never been married," he told me, and when I asked him why, he told me he had nearly tied the knot not long ago. "We came this close," he said, holding his fingers together, "but I realized that she was too argumentative. But she was a wonderful woman. She would bring a gun to a fistfight." "What do you mean?" I asked. "She would bring out the daggers over everything, like a knife, and go after me for anything and everything. If I just said I was mowing the lawn, she would get mad and argue. She was a wonderful woman, though. Over the years, we grew close and she knew everything about me and then would throw it in my face when she got mad, which was often. She used her verbal skills to manipulate me. My parents were divorced and it really affected me and my brother. I just didn't want my heart to harden like that, with my ex-girlfriend. I was afraid that with her anger and manipulation, I would grow apart from her and stop loving her. She was a wonderful woman, though."

I thought about what Bruce said and realized that women are constantly upset or going after men regarding physical abuse because men are often physically stronger. But women are often verbally more skilled and more ready to manipulate others using these verbal skills. Men aren't taught how to fight back verbally nor do they often want to; for some, it is not their nature. Men like Bruce would rather live the single life than have to spend their years being battered verbally without any recourse, since the laws and culture favor women and see men who cannot stand up for themselves as unworthy of sympathy, as wimps who can't "man up" and stay in control.

However, in today's society, manipulating a woman the way this girlfriend was manipulating and verbally berating Bruce would be seen as psychologically abusive if he responded in kind, and many men don't have the stomach for it. Notice how he kept almost apologizing for his feelings by stating over and over how wonderful his ex had been. He didn't feel able to say negative things about his ex. Rather than live in emotional pain without psychological and legal backup, many men, like Bruce, simply prefer to stay single.

While many men are taking a good look at the psychological and legal risks of marriage for themselves in this post-feminist era, many are also taking notice of the risks and lack of incentives of fatherhood. For it is not only in marriage that men have few rights but also many responsibilities; fatherhood and reproductive rights for men are also few and far between. And while reproduction may seem like an area more suited for women than men, nothing could be further from the truth. Paternity laws, the lack of choices that men have in their decisions for parenthood, and issues surrounding child support are also giving men cause to question whether they are full-fledged citizens in our society, or second-class citizens who are forced into involuntary servitude by the state and the women who profess to have once loved them.

In addition to gyms and bars in various areas of the country, I spent some time in Los Angeles and had the chance to talk with men and some women about men and marriage. As I was strolling through stores in Santa Monica one day, I found another research victim, Chris, who was a shoe salesman in his thirties. We started chatting about shoes, of course, but when he learned I was a psychologist writing a book about why men don't want to get married, he promptly stated, "You could be writing about me; I don't want to get married." "Why not?" I asked, and he replied, "There is nothing in it for me, no incentive and no reason. For instance, even if we had a pre-nup, it would mean nothing." Chris was concerned about the legal nature of marriage and that if he made a mistake, he would pay dearly without the law or the culture on his side.

I also met Gavin, a forty-year-old man, at an L.A. restaurant while meeting friends for dinner. He arrived with them and was seated next to me. "I just got married last week," he announced to the table full of pundits and filmmakers. "Really?" I said, "What made you decide to do that? What are some reasons that men get married in your mind?" "I turned forty and I was tired of running around, but mainly a man gets married because a woman wants to and you are afraid you will lose her." That kind of sounds more like blackmail to me, but okay. What I found interesting was that Gavin married a woman who was thirty-two years old and talked about how time was running out if they wanted to have kids. The other men at the table agreed that marrying a woman past thirty-five if you wanted kids was pushing it.

This age-related reality was hitting home with some of the women I met in L.A. For example, one beautiful lawyer I met who was almost forty years old disagreed with me that men did not want to marry. "All the men I know do want to get married. They are in their late thirties and want to marry someone in their twenties." Okay, the guys in their thirties just don't want to marry *her*. They wait until they are forty to find someone younger. Another complaint this lawyer had was that the girlfriends she had who were married had husbands who rarely worked and stayed home while the woman brought home the paycheck. "I don't want a man like that," the lawyer stated. The lawyer also broke up with one of her ex-boyfriends because he was too feminine. "I am a masculine woman but I still need someone who is more masculine than me."

What this lawyer doesn't seem to understand is that when masculinity is frowned upon and belittled in every aspect of society from the media to the classroom, men start to internalize the message. Our society tells men they are worthless perverts who reek of male privilege while simultaneously castrating them should they act in a manly manner, and now women are upset because men are becoming more feminized? You reap what you sow.

CHAPTER 2

My Body, My Choice— Your Body, No Choice

NO CHOICE TO CONSENT TO FATHERHOOD

We are already moving toward a society in which women have colonized reproduction, along with childrearing, and men will have less and less incentive to participate fully in family life and more and more penalties if any problems arise.

—Paul Nathanson and Katherine K. Young
in *Legalizing Misandry*[1]

Men's rights are very much dependent on how honest she chooses to be.

—Michael Higdon, Professor of Family Law,
The University of Tennessee

I often see cars with female drivers who have bumper stickers that proclaim "My body, my choice" or "Keep your laws off my body," and I wince. Why? Because the owner of the bumper sticker probably has no idea of the hypocrisy of her statement. I looked up the "My body, my choice" bumper stickers online and the first site I came to had the following as a description for the sticker:

The Constitution says that the government may not seize our persons, our bodies. That's why, when it comes to personal decisions like reproduction, it's my body, my choice.[2]

The *Irregular Times* site describes itself as a "liberal button and sticker shop." My guess is that the only issue they are liberal about is their own reproductive freedom; when it comes to men, liberal women and the white knights who support them are more than happy to throw this slogan under the bus. As Warren Farrell makes clear in *The Myth of Male Power*, although it's his body, a man has no choice when it comes to deciding whether or not to be a dad. He states:

> In the 1990s, if a woman and man make love and she says she is using birth control but is not, she has the right to raise the child without his knowing he even has a child, and then to sue him for retroactive child support even ten to twenty years later (depending on the state). This forces him to take a job with more pay and more stress and therefore earlier death. . . . He has the option of being a slave (working for another without pay or choice) or being a criminal. *Roe v. Wade* gave women the vote over their bodies. Men still don't have the vote over theirs—whether in love or war.[3]

Though this book will not get into the issue of the draft or war, it will tackle the area of love where it seems that men are as behind as they ever were. Many men, particularly young ones like Max in the last chapter, have no idea what their rights are (very few) until it's too late. Boys and men are rarely taught about their paternity rights, reproductive rights, or obligation to pay child support.

Yes, it is true that girls and women might not have formal classes or information in these areas, but there are many organizations such as Planned Parenthood or the National Organization for Women (NOW) that have very active groups involved in every area of politics and women have laws such as the Violence Against Women Act (VAWA) that protect them specifically as a group, even though many of the ways they are protected are at the expense of men's civil rights and due process. Women are also protected under the law when it comes to reproduction by abortion laws and other laws that look out for their interests.

For example, courts almost exclusively favor the mother and force men to pay child support to mothers regardless of whether she used false information or made false statements to the man concerning birth control.[4] Because women are given special privilege under the law when it comes to reproduction and men are held fully responsible for their acts, it is very important for

men, and teen males and their parents, to educate themselves in regard to paternity rights and child custody in
order to make informed decisions. As the book *Legalizing Misandry* points out:

> ... fatherhood can be a nightmare—legal, financial,
> and emotional—due to the laws governing divorce,
> custody, and access. These laws are not going to
> prevent all men from investing in family life, cer-
> tainly not those who consider marriage a religious
> covenant, but they have already made many other
> men think twice before becoming involved in what
> could easily become a no-win situation. Why invest
> so heavily in family life after all, if your children can
> be taken away from you or even turned against you
> so easily?[5]

And that is what can happen if you want your child or
children. What if you had no say in becoming a dad?
There are some nightmare situations that all men
should be aware of, such as becoming a father as a result
of trickery or rape. Yes, men and boys can be raped or
coerced into sex by women, though many people think
otherwise.

I once wrote an article asking if a man could be raped
by a woman, and the answers I received were shock-
ing, to say the least. Many of the commenters felt that
men were asking for it, should keep their legs crossed,

or should have known better than to allow a woman to harm them.[6] This sounds like what women used to be told about rape fifty or more years ago. Are men now being treated like the women of yesteryear? That's an interesting thought, but let's turn to educating ourselves on the responsibilities for those boys or men who become fathers without their consent.

Thankfully, there are educators out there like Professor Michael J. Higdon, who teaches at the University of Tennessee Law School and brings these cases to light. Higdon has an article on this topic titled "Fatherhood by Conscription: Nonconsensual Insemination and the Duty of Child Support."[7] In the article, Higdon describes three different cases of men who have been forced to be fathers against their will. One case involves a young man only fifteen years old named Nathaniel, who had sex with a thirty-four-year-old woman, Ricci, about five times. The woman got pregnant and, although in the state of California a minor under the age of sixteen cannot consent to sex, the court saw fit to force Nathaniel to pay child support to the woman who committed statutory rape against him.[8]

In another case Higdon highlights, an Alabama man, S.F., attended a party at the home of a female friend, T.M. He arrived intoxicated and passed out on her couch for the night. He was in her sole care and, when he awoke the next morning, he found all of his clothes removed except his unbuttoned shirt. According to Higdon:

Over the next few months, T.M. would openly boast to several people about how she had engaged in sexual intercourse with S.F. while he was unconscious. She would even go so far as to describe the evening as one that had "saved her a trip to the sperm bank." T.M. did in fact give birth to a child, and genetic testing confirmed that S.F. was the biological father.[9]

The last case that Higdon presents is that of Emile, who is from Louisiana and in 1983 was visiting his sick parents at the hospital. One evening while he was at the hospital, a nurse named Debra offered to perform oral sex on him, but only if he wore a condom. After the act was complete, Debra offered to get rid of the condom filled with Emile's sperm and must have impregnated herself, because nine months later genetic testing showed that Emile was the father of her baby. "The two never had sexual intercourse, only the one instance of oral sex with a condom."[10]

The commonality in these three cases was that a man or boy was forced into fatherhood against his will and was then forced by the court against his will to pay child support. Can you imagine the uproar if a fifteen-year-old girl had sex with a thirty-four-year-old man and she was obligated in any way to him by the courts? Or if a woman passed out at a party and a man had sex with her and she was then forced to have the baby? As Warren Farrell says about reproductive rights for men:

**He realizes that when a woman and he have cre-
ated a pregnancy, the issue is not the rights of
the female vs. the fetus, but the rights of the female, the fetus, and the father.** He realizes that a
woman who says "It's my body, it's my business," and
then chooses to have a child that she makes him pay
for; forces him to take a job he might like less just
because it pays more; forces him to stress himself out
and die early—forces him to use his body for eighteen years. If it's his body being used for eighteen
years, and his body dying sooner, shouldn't it be his
business, too? Isn't two decades of a man's life worth
nine months of a woman's?[11]

And if men's lives aren't worth much to the courts, the
life of a boy who has been sexually assaulted by a woman
is worth even less. Higdon reports that there are "numerous cases in which an adult woman became pregnant
as a result of sexual relations she initiated with a minor child."[12] However, every time the question arises of
whether a male victim of statutory rape should be made
liable for child support, *"every single court has answered
it in the affirmative—holding that yes, the minor father is
liable."*[13]

Now the boy has been victimized twice: once by the
woman who abused him, and again by the courts for the
next eighteen years while he engages in involuntary servitude to pay for a child that the law claimed he was not

even able to consent to at the time. Does anyone care about the psychological abuse they heap on a kid like this? Of course not; he's male and probably deserves it. After all, he asked for it, just like the girl who was asking to be raped by wearing a short skirt. Again, I ask, is it still 1950 and are boys the new girls?

What about a female who was the victim of a sexual assault: Would she, like her male counterpart, be held liable for the support of her children? Of course not. Reproductive rights are for women. Higdon highlights the case of *DCSE/Ester M.C. v. Mary L*, where a mother refused to provide support for her three minor children because they "were the product and result of an incestuous relationship with her brother" and as such "it was not a voluntary decision on her part to have children."[14]

The court ruled that "[i]f the sexual intercourse which results in the birth of a child is involuntary or without actual consent, a *mother* may have 'just cause' . . . for failing or refusing to support such a child."[15] I thought that it was all about the "best interests of the child" when it came to child support in the United States. Apparently, that's only if the parent is male. As the saying goes, "women have rights; men have responsibilities." Not only are men responsible for kids whom they didn't consent to fathering, but they are also responsible for kids whom are not even theirs genetically.

NO CHOICE IN PATERNITY LAW

For men, there are no reproductive benefits to marriage anymore.
—Blogger Mike T., reflecting on state-sanctioned paternity fraud[16]

If the genes don't fit . . . you must acquit.
—Signature line of Carnell Smith, advocate
for men accused of paternity fraud[17]

Sadly, paternity fraud is so rampant that it is hard to get
an exact count of how many men are either acting as
fathers to kids they think are their own or being forced
to pay child support after having been wrongly told that
they are the fathers to children that are not theirs.

According to the organization Fathers and Families:

> . . . tens of thousands of men have been wrongly as-
> signed paternity and are compelled by law to pay years
> of child support for children whom DNA tests have
> shown are not theirs. In many cases, the men have had
> little or no contact with the children they're required
> to support, and some had no idea they were "fathers"
> until their wages were garnished for child support.[18]

In 2007, *Men's Health Magazine* ran an article asking,
"Are You Raising Another Man's Child?" The article
states that "more than a million American men are in-
vesting their love, time, and money in a child who isn't

their own. But the worst part about this betrayal? How many people may be in on it."[19] The article comes up with the number of more than a million men by taking a look at studies on what it calls paternal discrepancy, which is defined as follows:

> Paternity fraud emphasizes the financial aspect of the phenomenon, but paternal discrepancy (PD) describes the anomaly itself—the disconnect between what men think is true and the genetic reality.[20]

The article finds the estimate of more than a million men by looking at studies of PD:

> After recently reviewing 67 studies on the subject, University of Oklahoma researchers found that PD rates tend to be much higher among men who have reason to believe there's been more than one dog in the yard. No surprise there. But leave out these men and you end up with a number that can safely be assumed to represent the rest of us. That number is 3.85 percent. Another review of 19 studies by a group at Liverpool John Moores University backs this up, putting the figure at 3.7 percent of dads. It may not seem like a lot—until you do the math. According to a 2005 U.S. Census Bureau report, there are 27,940,000 fathers nationwide with a child under 18. That means over a million guys out there are taking care of some other man's kid.[21]

Paternal discrepancy, paternity fraud. Call it what you will; it's all bad news for the large numbers of men out there who are affected. And not only are they betrayed by their wives or girlfriends, but there is also a whole industry of professionals in the medical profession who do not see it as their duty to inform the "father" that the child is not theirs.

Of course, lying is nothing new in the world of medicine. As late as 1970, doctors infamously withheld cancer diagnoses "for the good of the patient." (After all, they figured, these patients were doomed anyway, so what good would knowing do them?) This ended when it collectively dawned on doctors that, good intentions notwithstanding, paternalism was probably not the best approach. But given the nondisclosure policy of most genetic counselors these days, it might as well be 1970 again—except that now, with women dominating 92 percent of the field, paternalism seems to have been replaced by maternalism.[22]

Many of these female genetic counselors are concerned with how the *mother* would feel if her husband found out the truth, not the poor duped dad, of course. Talk about a good old girl's network. But since no one cares much about men's emotions in these cases—there is little formal research on the emotional damage that paternity fraud has on men—and states just care about extracting money from any man possible, not much is being done to combat paternity fraud.

The emotional stakes and feelings of betrayal have to be very high for a man who finds out a child is not his. In many cases of married men, men who found out they were not the father of a child were devastated and never really got over the shock. Many had trouble with depression, but, for most men, the feeling is anger, which is often said to be depression turned outward. This anger is a common feeling for many men, as you will see from some of my informal research.

Since there is a dearth of formal research on men's emotional reactions after finding out a child they thought was theirs was not, I decided to conduct my own informal poll[23] on my blog at PJ Media and ask men about their feelings on paternity fraud. Here is the question I posed and the resulting responses:

> If you found out tomorrow that your five-year-old son or daughter was not yours and that you were also liable for another 13 years of child support for that child, how would you feel?
>
> ☐ I wouldn't care.
>
> ☐ Anger and fury at the mother.
>
> ☐ Depression; I would have a hard time coping with the news.

□ Anger and depression.

□ Glad my genes weren't passed along and hope that the biological dad's were genetically superior.

□ None of the above.

□ Angry at the system that forced me to pay.

□ Other.

The question must have hit a nerve as more than 3,200 male readers responded to the poll and the following results were found: 2 percent "didn't care"; 36 percent felt "anger and fury at the mother"; 6 percent felt "depression"; 18 percent felt "anger and depression"; 0 said they were glad their "genes weren't passed along"; 2 percent said "none of the above"; 32 percent were "angry at the system that forced them to pay"; and finally 5 percent said "other."[24] The most interesting part of the informal poll was the comments. Here are some examples of how men felt:

Joe in Houston says:
This did happen to me. I was angry at the mother. He wasn't 5, as in the poll, he was 11. At first I still wanted to raise him, but after the ex continued taunting me by telling him how I wasn't his father, I severed all ties to the boy. Some may see this as a failing, I see it as self-preservation, and to those that ask the question of whether or not the courts will make a non-biological

parent pay child support, pay attention, YES THEY WILL! YES THEY WILL! They see you as nothing more than a source of cash for the child. It seems that a person in these situations should be able to sue the real father for child support.[25]

tiger6 states:

I pretty much agree with the sentiments already here. Assuming the mother had lied to me, I'm angry with her for cheating on me AND putting me into a position where the state can force me to pay. The state screwing me over I'm mad at, but have come to expect. SHE was supposed to love me and not put me in that position.

But still, if a judge ordered me to pay child support on a child I knew wasn't mine . . . I would be tempted to tell him to just put me in jail right now because I simply would not pay. I can't say I would do that for sure, but it's at least my first instinct.[26]

Difster states:

Point of note for commenters, in many states, after a certain amount of time you can no longer contest paternity and be forced to pay child support anyway because "someone has to do it."

That being said, I would split with the mother if it didn't already happen and do everything I could, probably including outright fraud to get full custody of that child. I wouldn't punish the child for the actions of the mother and instead of paying, I'd rather just raise the kid myself as my own and kick the mother out of the picture. I wouldn't resort to violence, but I'd do a heck of a frame job to make sure she ended up in jail for something.[27]

Old Guy says:
I wanted to choose both anger at the mother for making me a patsy and anger at the system that would still force me to pay. One more example of how men are oppressed by the Matriarchy.[28]

Cthulhu says:
So, you've been going along raising a kid for five years.... Chances are, you've somewhat bonded with him or her—and we're talking about an innocent child. But you just found out that the mother had been lying to you for five years about the parentage—there's room for some anger and betrayal with her, but you might work it out. But to be treated as a cash cow by the state for an additional 13 years regardless of your continuing relationship with mother or child? "Outrage" doesn't begin to cover it.[29]

TeeJaw says:
Cthulhu says what I was thinking. The anger and disappointment at the mother, the anger at the system

that has inserted itself in the whole thing would be enough to deal with, but also that I probably would have bonded deeply with the child. I would feel like running away to a south sea island where I would never have to see any of them again. One thing sure, there would be a boatload of compassion heaped on the mother and child and absolutely none on the cuckold husband, who would be seen as nothing more than an ATM machine.[30]

So the most common responses to paternity fraud from the polltakers was anger at the mother who put the man in this position and anger at the state that forces him to pay for a child that is not his. These are good and appropriate responses because they are the fuel that will cause men to act on their own behalf to change the laws.

Remember that in the introduction, I mentioned that men's rights activist Warren Farrell says two ingredients are necessary for a major movement: emotional rejection and economic hurt. Paternity fraud has these two ingredients written all over it.

Luckily, there are activists who are out there fighting to change the laws that force men to pay for children that are not their own, even if they find out years later. This is what happened to a friend of State Senator Stacey Campfield, and it gave him the courage and impetus to try to change the antiquated laws in Tennessee that force a man to pay for another man's child against his will. His friend found out that he was not the father of a young child whom he was raising. Once his friend came forward, Campfield says he has also heard from numerous Tennessee men who have been the victims of paternity fraud and he believes that fairness in the law is important as "people lose faith in the system and think that cheating is the only answer."[31]

Campfield is no ordinary politician; controversy is his middle name. The local weekly alternative in Knoxville, the *Metro Pulse*, ran a front-page story asking the question, "What the Heck Is Wrong with Stacey Campfield?" In the article, it mentions that Campfield has (gasp!):

> . . . proposed a range of legislation on things like child support, orders of protection, and sexual-abuse allegations, that, as a Nashville scene blogger put it a few weeks ago, seem to derive from a sense "that women are crazy lying bitches men need protecting from." . . . And yet, it is hard to escape the contradictions underlying his geniality. He is a family-values conservative who has never married, a fathers' rights advocate with no children.[32]

So, is the article implying that politicians or activists are only normal if they fight for the rights of those who are just like them? I sure hope not, because there would be fewer rights for women, African Americans, gays and many others if the only activists allowed in the fight were those who met the criteria of the group whose rights they were fighting for. And frankly, given that much legislation in the area of family law and domestic violence makes guys out to be potential drunken louts out to rape, beat or abandon women, why all the outcry? After all, what's good for the goose is good for the gander, as the saying goes.

Luckily, Campfield feels some sense of duty to men who are the victims of paternity fraud who are being forced to pay child support for kids who are not theirs. Jesse Fox Mayshark, the writer of the *Metro Pulse* article on Campfield, sums up the criticism by opponents of such a bill:

> The child support bill, the criticism of it was that it could actually harm children. If you withdraw one parent's support but you don't necessarily have that other biological parent there providing support, the child ends up with less support.[33]

To which Campfield replies:

> You can say the same thing about someone who might be in prison for a crime they didn't commit. The victim may feel wonderful that there's a person in prison, but if that person has been proven by DNA evidence they didn't do whatever, then I don't think it's fair that we should hold them behind bars for a crime they didn't commit.[34]

No, it's not fair, and Campfield put forth a bill to the Tennessee state legislature to try to change the law:

> (n) Upon application of either party, the court shall decree a termination of support when scientific tests to determine parentage of the child or children, or to establish paternity in another person, are performed and such tests exclude the obligor from parentage of such child or children. The results of such parentage testing shall only be admitted into evidence in accordance with the procedures established in §§ 24-7-112.

Campfield also emailed me with a follow-up to this bill:

> Helen, here is a copy of the bill as amended (the second document). I am having another bill drafted to compliment [*sic*] this one. In cases where this happens the original "father" can go after the real biological father for the back child support payments that were paid as part of the original child support agreement.[35]

The bill passed the House of Representatives in Tennessee but unfortunately failed in the Senate. However, there is good news. In October 2012, Stacey let me know that there was a victory for DNA victims in the state of Tennessee.[36] He wrote on his blog:

The State Supreme court has just ruled unanimously
a person mislead into believing they are the father of
a child may sue the mother for back payments made
if it is later found they are not the biological father
of that child.

I tried to pass a piece of watered down legislation
a few years ago when the Democrats were in power
that would have allowed the non biological father to
stop making future payments on their non child. It
went down in spectacular flames.[37]

It's amazing what can happen with persistence and a
little luck.

There are other states that are adopting bills per-
taining to paternity fraud that increase the chances of
fairness for men. For example, Georgia passed a paternity fraud bill that gives men the right to terminate
child support if they file a paternity test showing zero
percent chance that they are the father, and if they also
meet other conditions.[38] Carnell Smith, an engineer
in Decatur, Georgia, who was a victim of paternity
fraud, started a group called U.S. Citizens Against Paternity Fraud that lobbied for the law in Georgia and
won.[39] Smith is a true advocate for men's rights and
has been involved in getting paternity laws enacted for
men in twenty-nine states.[40] His story is told in more
detail in the last chapter of this book on "Fighting
Back."

But until paternity fraud is treated as a serious issue and men are protected in *all* states, there is still much work to do. Men still have few choices when they are lied to about the paternity of their children and forced to pay child support for kids who aren't theirs, but they can also encounter the boot of the state against their neck just as severely or even more so if they do not pay for children who are theirs, as we will see in the next section.

NO CHOICE IN PAYING CHILD SUPPORT (AND JAIL TIME TO BOOT)

Across the U.S. on an average day, roughly 50,000 persons are in jail or in prison for sex-payment debt.
—Douglas Galbi[41]

We can probably expect that most of those persons in jail for child support nonpayments are male, since the majority of child support is paid by men and law enforcement is reluctant to put women in jail. Custodial fathers make up only about 17.8 percent of custodial parents in the United States,[42] leaving more than 82 percent as noncustodial parents who would be responsible for the bulk of child support. In an article at MSNBC.com, the author notes that many of the men who cannot pay child support and end up in jail are poor and had not even talked to an attorney prior to being imprisoned:

"Languishing in jail for weeks, months, and sometimes over a year, these parents share one trait...besides their poverty: They went to jail without ever talking to an attorney," according to the lawsuit filed by the non-profit Southern Center of Human Rights in Atlanta.

While jailing non-paying parents—the vast majority of them men—does lead to payment in many cases, critics say that it unfairly penalizes poor and unemployed parents who have no ability to pay, even though federal law stipulates that they must have "willfully" violated a court order before being incarcerated.

They compare the plight of such parents to the poor people consigned to infamous "debtors' prisons" before such institutions were outlawed in the early 1800s.[43]

And if jail is not bad enough, due process and the Constitution are thrown out the window when it comes to men and their inability to pay child support:

The ability of judges to jail parents without a trial is possible because failure to pay child support is usually handled as a civil matter, meaning that the non-custodial parent—or the "contemnor" in legal terms—is found guilty of contempt of court and ordered to appear at a hearing.

He or she is not entitled to some constitutional protections that criminal defendants receive, including the presumption of innocence. And in five states—Florida, Georgia, Maine, South Carolina and Ohio—one of the omitted protections is the right to an attorney.[44]

No one ever makes this point, but one of the reasons that this type of atrocity is allowed to happen is that it is men who are thrown in jail. Yes, occasionally a woman may be jailed to make a point, but not often. Our society is not that willing to throw women in jail or strip them of their Constitutional rights. Some estimates find that up to 52 percent of men will be arrested at some point in their lives, and that a man is about four times as likely as a woman to be arrested.[45] I was once in a continuing education class of psychologists where the speaker asked how many of the men in the audience had been arrested. More than one third raised their hands. If you don't believe me, ask twenty male friends or colleagues if they have ever been arrested for any reason, and you may be surprised at the answer. I have dealt with male clients sent for evaluation by the courts or their attorneys who have been jailed or had family members (all male) in jail for child support payments or false domestic violence charges. These men don't seem upset because of learned helplessness in dealing with a justice system that views their bodies as belonging to the state in matters of family law.

Add to jail time the fact that in many states there

are other penalties for not paying child support, such as losing driving privileges, professional licenses and passport privileges.[46] So now, you can't get around, you can't work and you can't even leave the country if you are a dad who can't or won't engage in involuntary servitude. At the beginning of this chapter, I discussed the bumper sticker that pro-choice women stick on their cars that read, "My body, my choice." All I can do is shake my head and think "what hypocrites." Women in the United States can decide whether to be a mother, can have a child and in some states give it up for adoption without even informing the father, and can use men for eighteen years—and sometimes more—to pay for their children. Men have no say in reproduction. Maybe now you understand why the "My body, my choice" bumper sticker has a hollow ring to it.

With so many men in jail or suffering to pay child support, is it any reason that younger men are reluctant to get too involved with marriage and fatherhood? Add the potential for eighteen years of involuntary servitude and it's no wonder that some men are going on strike or no longer putting their all into a career, which brings us to the next chapter on the college strike.

CHAPTER 3

The College Strike

Where the Boys Aren't

WELCOME TO "GIRLINGTON"

> *Young men are not going to whine about their predicament.*
> *They are not going to organize workshops or support groups.*
> *(Thank goodness.) Teenage boys are the one group of Americans*
> *who do not like to gather in circles and talk about grievances*
> *and misgivings. So what will they do? My guess is that vast*
> *numbers will just stop trying and withdraw. It would not be*
> *an organized strike—it would just happen. It is happening.*[1]
> —Christina Hoff Sommers, in an interview with the author

Imagine that women were taking flight from the nation's universities and colleges; we would have a national uproar. When men flee, it's worth a mention every once in a while and there is a bit of hand-wringing over what effect their apathy will have on women. Who will they date? Who will they marry? Will the men be good enough for them? What about hypergamy? Women need to marry up, so the men better man up, get educated and make plenty of money to make women feel more secure. But it seems that many men are no longer going along with the plan. Some have given up on college as it has become a "finishing school for women," and others never had the chance to consider it as they became disconnected from school a long time ago.

How many women versus men are in college? In Christina Hoff Sommers' provocative book *The War Against Boys*, written in 2000, the numbers were already taking a nosedive and had been for many years before that. Sommers notes that in 1996, there were 8.4 million women enrolled in college but only 6.7 million men enrolled in college. She adds that the U.S. Department of Education predicted that by 2007, there would be 9.2 million women in college and 6.9 million men.[2] What was the actual number of men and women in 2007? I looked up the National Center for Education statistics for fall enrollment by degree-granting institutions and found that there was a total of 7.816 million men enrolled and 10.432 million women. In 2009, there were 11.658 million women enrolled and 8.769 million men.[3] Here is what the National Center for Education statistics says about men enrolled in postbaccalaureate programs:

Since 1988, the number of females in postbaccalaureate programs have exceeded the number of males. Between 2000 and 2010, the number of male full-time postbaccalaureate students increased by 38 percent, compared with a 62 percent increase in the number of females. Among part-time postbaccalaureate students, the number of males increased by 17 percent and the number of females increased by 26 percent.[4]

In terms of percentages of men and women enrolled in college, Kay Hymowitz notes that "women between the ages of 25 and 34 with a bachelor's degree or higher outnumber men. This started in the 1980s and the trends continue to be in women's favor. Between 1975 and 2006, the percentage of women with at least a college degree increased from 18.6 to 34.2 percent. Men barely budged: their numbers went from 26.8 percent to 27.9."[5]

Today the number of women is 58 percent and predictions are that women will reach 60 percent of the college grads in the near future.[6] In some colleges, the percentages are already nearing 60 percent; for example, schools like North Carolina at Chapel Hill or private schools like NYU have almost reached the 60 percent mark already. The University of Vermont in Burlington has so many women that the women jokingly call their college town Girlington.

The *New York Times* had an article looking at the prospects for women on these girl-dominated campuses and it did, indeed, look pretty grim. Women are going out and partying by themselves:

After midnight on a rainy night last week in Chapel Hill, N.C., a large group of sorority women at the

University of North Carolina squeezed into the corner booth of a gritty basement bar. Bathed in a neon glow, they splashed beer from pitchers, traded jokes and belted out lyrics to a Taylor Swift heartache anthem thundering overhead. As a night out, it had everything—except guys.[7]

So where are all the men? According to the *New York Times* article:

Women have represented about 57 percent of enrollments at American colleges since at least 2000, according to a recent report by the American Council on Education. Researchers there cite several reasons: women tend to have higher grades; men tend to drop out in disproportionate numbers; and female enrollment skews higher among older students, low-income students, and black and Hispanic students.[8]

This *New York Times* article is very typical of media accounts of why men aren't attending college in as great numbers as women; there is little insight into why this is happening, or there is some anti-male, pro-female reason that boils down to men being lazy and dumb and women being smart and studious. Why are men getting worse grades; why do they tend to drop out of school in disproportionate numbers? Maybe if the media and elites weren't so openly pleased that women are outpacing men in college, they might be more interested in why men are fleeing the campus. Their PC agenda has been years in the making and its casualties are men and their education and, in many ways, society. But don't look to the media or elites to change the culture; we must do it ourselves. To figure out how to motivate men to go to college, we must first understand why they went on strike in the first place and what kinds of changes must be made to keep the college environment guy-friendly.

IS THERE A WAR AGAINST MEN AND BOYS IN EDUCATION?

> *When will it be fair? When women are 60 percent or 75 percent of college enrollments? Perhaps it will be fair when there are no men at all.*
> —Diane Ravitch, fellow at the Brookings Institution and former assistant secretary of education[9]

The college strike didn't happen overnight. It started years ago when the war against boys began after the feminist era. Initially, feminism was presented as being about equal rights between the sexes. Now it is often about revenge and special privileges for women and girls. Christina Hoff Sommers is a scholar at the American Enterprise Institute in Washington, D.C., and she has keen insight into the plight of American boyhood. In her book, *The War Against Boys*, Sommers explains in detail the efforts of feminists and their sycophants to turn the educational system into one that favors girls at the expense of boys. Boys and their masculine traits and needs are often frowned upon in U.S. schools, and boys are now seen as "defective girls" in need of a major overhaul.

According to Sommers, "gender experts at Harvard, Wellesley, and Tufts, and in the major women's organizations, believe that boys and men in our society will remain sexist (and potentially dangerous) unless socialized away from conventional maleness. . . . The belief that boys are being wrongly 'masculinized' is inspiring a movement to 'construct boyhood' in ways that will render boys less competitive, more emotionally expressive, more nurturing—more, in short, like girls."[10] Boys are the gender most at risk in the U.S. educational system, yet little help is forthcoming. Sommers refers to a number of studies in her book to make the point that boys are having more trouble in schools than girls.

For example, a MetLife study stated, "Contrary to the commonly held view that boys are at an advantage over girls in school, girls appear to have an advantage over boys in terms of their future plans, teacher's expectations, everyday experiences at school and interactions in the classroom."[11] Boys are less engaged in school, and less engagement means less success in the classroom; in fact, engagement with school is probably the single most important factor of academic success.[12] The Department of Education was already documenting boys' lack of commitments to school back in the 1980s and 1990s. Boys are more likely than girls to come to school without supplies and without doing their homework.[13] Sommers reports that until we reengage boys by improving their study habits and get them more interested in learning and achievement, more girls than boys will go to college.

Why aren't boys more engaged in school? According to Sommers, "schools today tend to be run by women for girls. Classrooms can be hostile environments for boys. They like action, competition and adventure stories. Those are not in favor. Games like tag and dodge-ball are out; tug of war has become tug of peace, and male heroes have been replaced by Girl Power."[14] Boys even receive lower marks by female teachers according to research done for the London School of Economic's Centre for Economic Performance.[15] Boys now feel no connection to school, because they are square pegs being forced into a round hole. I should note that some girls may feel this way also.

However, if girls are uninterested in school, there is always an outcry, just like there has been over girls' "lack of self-esteem" in the schools over the years—though honestly, girls' self-esteem has never seemed higher and, frankly, *exceptionally high* self-esteem is not necessarily a good thing. Robyn Dawes, a professor of psychology, says, "The false belief in self-esteem as a major force for good cannot potentially, but actually be harmful."[16]

However, disinterest in school for boys can be a real problem. I found that even in my own studies of violent teens, boys' and girls' disengagement from school is a serious issue and resulted in more violence.[17]

For normal boys, this disinterest may take the form of no plans to further their education, dropping out of school or just not going to college. No one really cares, and some feminist types even say it's fine that older boys and men don't get a college education because they can make it without one. Maybe so for some, but for many more, they will fall between the cracks either sitting home or getting nowhere in a career. According to Sommers, "a college education is crucial to a young person's economic prospects. But colleges have become far more congenial places for females than males. There is now a large and growing cohort of young men who are not going to find a place for themselves in the new information-economy. Good construction and manufacturing jobs are gone. The military? Many young men are too overweight or too undermotivated for that."[18]

And though it is not clear that college and higher education or lack thereof is the *main* reason men are losing ground economically, it can't be helping that many are forgoing future earnings by skipping school. College-educated people generally earn a higher wage than those who do not go to college. Take a look at the following graph in Figure 1 on median annual earnings for men, and note the declining incomes in general.

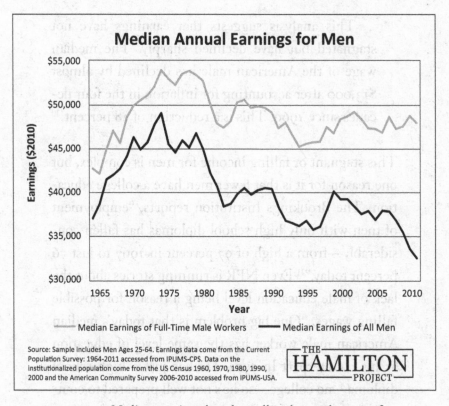

FIGURE 1. Median earnings based on all males aged twenty-five to sixty-four. *Source:* The Hamilton Project at the Brookings Institution.[19]

According to the Brookings Institution, which has been following men's wages for quite some time, in the graph shown in Figure 1:

> The figure plots the median earnings based on all males aged 25–64, along with the more conventional plot that is based only on those men aged 25–64 that happen to work full-time.

This analysis suggests that earnings have not stagnated but have declined sharply. The median wage of the American male has declined by almost $13,000 after accounting for inflation in the four decades since 1969. This is a reduction of 28 percent![20]

This stagnant or falling income for men is complex, but one reason for it is that fewer men have a college education. The Brookings Institution reports, "employment of men with only high school diplomas has fallen considerably—from a high of 97 percent in 1967 to just 76 percent today."[21] Even NPR is running stories about the lack of male education level being a reason for possible falling wages. "One big problem is that today's median American male worker has the same level of education as his counterpart in 1973. He has just a high school diploma—no college—so he's not well prepared to compete for better jobs."[22]

But rather than look in depth at why men are not getting the skills nor having the motivation they need to succeed at college, the media and experts such as the ones described in the introduction just announce that it's the boys' own fault that they are not doing well and that they are just immature and on their way to becoming the child-men of tomorrow. "Women are taking over because they have the right stuff. They are more likely to aspire to go to college than men," says Kay Hymowitz, author of *Manning Up*.[23] Boys, not so much. But the question today isn't why are women doing so well at school, but rather, why aren't men? They're the ones dropping out. What has changed over the past few decades that is causing them to drop out, give up or go on strike from the college track? Maybe it's the schools and the culture that are the problem, not necessarily the men.

ARE COLLEGES HOSTILE ENVIRONMENTS FOR MEN?

> *What explains this male flight? Let me speculate a bit and offer a reason that dare not speak its name in today's PC climate: universities are increasingly becoming feminized and many men, to use the antidiscrimination vocabulary, loathe a hostile working environment. In a word, males increasingly feel emasculated in today's universities.*
> —Robert Weissberg, Professor of Political Science[24]

In an article on the *Minding the Campus* website, Weissberg explains why so many men are fleeing from campuses around the country. Although he focuses on white males in the piece, the truth is that minority men are just as scarce, or maybe more so. According to Christina Hoff Sommers:

When economist Andrew Sum and his colleagues at the Center for Labor Market Studies at Northeastern University looked at gender disparities in the Boston

Public Schools, they found that for the class of 2008, among blacks, there were 188 females for every 100 males attending a four-year college or university. Among Hispanics the ratio was 233 female for every 100 males. For white students the gap was smaller, but still significant: 123 females to every 100 males.

The facts are incontrovertible: young women from low-income neighborhoods in Boston, Los Angeles or Washington, D.C., do much better than the young men from those same neighborhoods. There are now dozens of studies with titles like "The Vanishing Latino Male in Higher Education" and "African-American Males in Education: Endangered or Ignored?" A recent study by College Board on minority men found that among African American and Hispanic males 15–24 who do not pursue their education beyond high school, half of them "will end up unemployed, incarcerated or dead."[25]

But no men, minority or otherwise, are safe from sexism on campus. A commenter named Marcus weighed in on the *Minding the Campus* article on the white male shortage. He said, "As a black male I can testify that this is indeed what is happening on college campuses. White males are at the forefront of the academic sexism but they are definitely coming after all males. Believe it."[26] This hostile environment has been going on for years with little blowback. Many male professors are Uncle Tims (male sellouts) trying to make themselves look good to the feminists in their midst, and the male students are afraid to fight back for fear their grades will suffer. Men's activist Glenn Sacks encountered this dynamic firsthand at UCLA in the late 1990s when the hostilities against men ran deep. He summarized his thoughts in a column that highlights the question many men are asking themselves today more than ever:

> I thought of the feminist academics (female and male) who poured their derision upon them, knowing that their students could not effectively fight back. I thought of the timid male professors who were so content with their own careers that they were perfectly willing to allow 18 year-old boys to be beat up on rather than jeopardize their own comfort by speaking out. And I asked myself a question which hundreds of thousands of male college students often ask themselves: "What am I even doing here?"[27]

Many other men have asked themselves the same thing in today's current anti-male climate. "Michael," who is twenty-eight years old, wrote to me to tell me his story:

> I was a pretty smart kid, at least as far as the testing apparatus showed. I always scored in the 99th percentile on the FCAT, Florida's standardized state achievement test. In my junior year, I took the PSAT and became a National Merit Scholar; I was also awarded a Bright Futures Scholarship, which meant

that I basically had a free ticket to college. I enrolled in the University of Florida, transferred my 60-odd credit hours from my community college, and entered UF as a junior. Again, totally free ride: the scholarships paid for classes, books, room and board, and even pocket money. . . .

One of my professors was fascinated by me, in the way you might be fascinated by a bizarre animal that you don't understand; at one point, he announced (in front of the rest of the class) that I was surely socially maladjusted because my parents had spanked me when I was a child. At another point, during a dinner we were having together near the end of the semester, I made the mistake of conversationally mentioning that I planned on purchasing a firearm when I had finished with college and got out on my own. From the wide-eyed looks around the dinner table, you'd have thought I said I eat babies on a regular basis. Needless to say, the professor thought this was further evidence of my maladjustment.

I couldn't walk to class without passing at least one group of surly protestors every day. Sometimes more than one. You name it: protesting Taco Bell, protesting Israel, this and that, to the point where I felt like I was besieged on all sides perpetually—and that was even before I got into class for my daily dose of propaganda. Eventually I decided that I couldn't take it anymore. Free was too much to pay for this.

I washed my hands and dropped out; in the final car trip away from UF, with my belongings packed into the back of my mother's Jeep, she commented that she hadn't seen me look so happy since the first day she had dropped me off at college over a year before. That experience convinced me that college, if not quite a sham, was at least an exaggerated phenomenon, useful for hard sciences that require precision and years of study and practice. I went to college for one reason: because I was really smart and Smart People Go To College. It was preordained from the moment I ever took my first standardized test. I quickly discovered what an intellectual cesspool the liberal arts college was, to my dismay.

Nowadays, I work for a major telecom, and make about $50k a year. I'm certainly not rich—I'm barely middle class—but seeing as how I don't have anyone to care for but myself, I have a fine standard of living. I don't want for anything, I don't struggle to pay my bills, and—perhaps most importantly to me—I am completely, absolutely, 100% debt-free. Student loans certainly won't be dogging me for the rest of my days. I'm pretty happy with what I have right now, and I don't regret dropping out of UF at all. There's nothing they would have been able to teach me, in my line of study, that would have improved my job prospects or even made me any better at my signature talent of writing.[28]

On my blog, I asked about college experiences—negative or positive—and twenty-five-year-old "Andy" emailed me about his experiences. Andy also told me that he found college a hostile environment when he attended Wheelock College in Boston:

Once at the school, interactions with the staff got strange. I realized quickly, being a male, how much of a minority at that school I truly was. I'm a fairly conservative guy, I'd call myself Libertarian if that wasn't such a loaded term these days, and being with that sort of outlook at a predominantly female school that caters almost exclusively to people who want teaching degrees, in Boston, during the second Bush term, I was not well received. There were quite a few Female Issues and Female History classes, quite a few female-oriented extracurriculars and clubs, and, if I remember correctly, the first day that we were there, we had to sit through a presentation on avoiding sexual assault on campus, which was awkward for myself.

I took a Sociology course and we had regular debates on social issues. Without fail, on almost every debate it was myself on one side, and the rest of the class, all female, on the other. One particular debate was on the topic of abortion, on which I took the stance of "I personally would want to avoid it at all costs if I was in a relationship with a woman and the issue came up, but it's not my choice, it's the female's, and it's not my place to tell anyone else how to deal with that situation." I thought that stance was fair, and non-offensive, but the rest of the class made it very clear that I was in the wrong, and that I was a fairly terrible person for having any thoughts on the topic at all.

Wheelock College definitely had a Men = Bad attitude, and it made [my] time there awkward and difficult at times. I only spent a year there before moving to California to try and make it in the TV business (the closest I got was drunkenly writing a synopsis of a show where Rob Lowe played a PR consultant for a Military Contractor). After that, I was done with college. I have many memories of my time at Wheelock, most of them involve being called a Right-Wing bigot, getting kicked out of my dorm, and working at a local Quiznos. There are happy memories as well, but very few were facilitated by the Wheelock Staff.[29]

"John" also emailed in response to my request to write in about college experiences. John made the mistake of taking a college course with his fiancé and wrote to tell me about his experience:

My fiancé and I decided to take a class that would be a little less stressful, or so we thought, as an elective.

We, and I can't believe I admit to this, we took women and ethnic studies. Just as an aside, I'm a white, blonde male, and she's a white, black-haired woman.

The makeup of the class was 75% black, 97% female and 100% bullshit. The one other white male in the class and I learned early on that we were the target of all the animosity being discussed. I did my part and actually argued my voice and against the indoctrination, not getting that this was only digging my grave with the instructor. . . .

A running theme was the concept that since I am not part of a minority I cannot possibly understand what they've gone through, and that because of my being born a white male I was inherently in a privileged position. Another running theme was that minorities can't be racist. I said many times in that class that their theories were ridiculous and offensive. . . .

One female in particular seemed to take my viewpoints personally and began to attack me, both verbally in the classroom, then stalking me on the class's Internet discussion board. I told her and my instructor this was unacceptable behavior. The instructor did nothing, and the female, an immigrant from Africa via Germany, saw nothing wrong with her behavior.

I explained the situation to the dean of the university after months of trying to get in touch with her and I was told it wasn't her call and that she couldn't do anything about it. When I tried to take a medical absence for something unrelated, the university slapped me with a "needs anger management" class before I was allowed to re-attend, because that same lunatic complained I made her uncomfortable.

Needless to say, I had already been cautious around women, having grown up with Tawana Brawley in my backyard and daily stories of sexual harassment, I played it safe and passive every time. But it doesn't matter. The only way not to lose is to not play. So I'm out.

I'm Galt.[30]

"Jeff" wrote in with an interesting observation:

It comes down to one observation. Men must live a double life on campus. To succeed, men must believe one thing but act like they believe another. Manliness wants to compete, to win, to boast, to glory, even to fail honorably against the best. This is disallowed to men on campus. Winners are picked not discovered. It was clear to me; the winners would almost always be females and occasionally males who lived the double life. I left.[31]

Though most of the guys who wrote to me about bailing out of college seemed to go on and do well in life without a college degree, there are many guys out there who have withdrawn, are unemployed or underemployed, and aren't doing so well. Many who drop out of school or end up in jail are minorities who had few resources at school, partly because they were male and the skills they needed were not deemed important enough for the school system or culture to address. When organizations like the American Association of University Women put out research and programs to help girls, but dismiss boys' needs as unimportant, these are the consequences. Men who become uninterested or wary about school either don't go or find that higher education is not a good fit for many of the male gender.

Do the experiences of these four men represent the norm for young men arriving on campus? I decided that the best person to answer this question was Christina Hoff Sommers. I contacted her by email and she graciously agreed to be interviewed. Following are some of my questions and her thoughts on men and college:

HELEN SMITH: Men are attending college at lower rates now than even in 2000 when you wrote your book. Why do you think they are bailing out? Are they on strike? Does disengagement in school at an earlier age correlate to fewer men going to college? What about the notion that men are just going into the military or can get better jobs without a college degree? Does this ring true to you?

CHRISTINA HOFF SOMMERS: The moment a young man arrives on the college campus, he is treated as

a member of the suspect class. One popular freshman orientation program is called "She Fears You."
Next there are "Take Back the Night" marches, per-
formances of the *Vagina Monologues*—accusatory
posters plastered all around the school—and lots of
classroom readings—all driving home the point that
women are from Venus and men are from Hell.

Few classes are mandatory except freshman writing seminars. Unless the student is well-organized
(and what boy is?) he will be too late for the reasonable course offerings and end up in a class where he
has to read chick victim lit like the *Joy Luck Club* or
Girl Interrupted. A nightmare for many boys.

Are boys on strike? That is an interesting question. Young men are not going to whine about their
predicament. They are not going to organize work-
shops or support groups. (Thank goodness.) Teenage boys are the one group of Americans who do not
like to gather in circles and talk about grievances and
misgivings. So what will they do? My guess is that
vast numbers will just stop trying and withdraw. It
would not be an organized strike—it would just happen. It is happening.

HS: Can you explain Title IX and why it might be important to understand in men's uninterest in school?
Do you think the sports angle has kept men out of
programs that no longer offer team sports or have
gotten rid of them?

CHS: Colleges and universities with a severe short-age of men are looking for male-friendly innova-tions to attract them. One sure-fire way is to start a football team. Several colleges are doing just that—Utica in New York, Seton Hill in Pennsylvania, and Shenandoah in Virginia, for example. As Shenan-doah's athletic director told the *New York Times* in a 2006 interview, "You would be hard pressed to find five . . . marketing experts that could guarantee you 100 new, paying male students in one year. But you add five football coaches and they can do it. In fact they can find you 200 if you want." But here is the Catch 22: adding a football team to attract young men places your college at risk for a Title IX lawsuit. The law, as currently interpreted, requires schools with relatively few males to have comparably few male teams. But males, taken as a group, are far more interested in sports than females. Title IX prevents schools from using one of the most effective market-ing techniques to draw male applicants.

HS: Have sexual harassment laws and negative male stereotypes kept men from feeling comfortable at colleges? Do you think that activities such as "take back the night" make men feel like predators or un-comfortable?

CHS: The "Take Back the Night Marches" and the "fact sheets" that claim vast numbers of college women are being battered and raped by the males on their campus are part of an ideologically motivated campaign. There is a place for warning students about binge drinking, and teaching young men that they must behave as gentleman [*sic*]—but what we now have on campus is quite different. It's about accusing all males of original sin. Because of pressure from women's groups, the Department of Education has changed the regulations. It will now be easier for schools to find young men guilty of date rape—including many who are innocent.

HS: Do you think we need a men's center at some schools?

CHS: I am skeptical about men's centers. If history is any indication of the future, they would be run by gender activists who want to help "liberate" men from their masculinity. Few men are interested in that kind of help.

HS: What have you learned in the last ten years since writing *The War Against Boys*? Has much changed for the better or worse in terms of the war against boys and men?

CHS: I originally thought that once educators, legislators, and parents realized that boys were in trouble academically, our schools would try to make classrooms more accommodating to them. That has not happened.

Here is the problem in a nutshell. Because historically women have been the second sex, and did suffer discrimination, there is now an elaborate and powerful network of private and federal agencies that protect and promote women's interests. Boys do not have a lobby to defend them. Worse, the women's lobby (especially hard-line members like the American Association of University Women—AAUW) fights efforts to help boys.

Women's groups follow a double standard: When women lag behind men, that is an injustice that must be aggressively targeted. But when men are lagging behind women, that is a triumph of equity to be celebrated.

This double standard also extends to men's sex lives at college. Women are encouraged to explore their sexuality without consequence, while the men are held responsible for their sexual acts, often without due process. Young men think that they will go to college to meet young women and have a good time, but some of them have no idea what some of these schools have in store for them.

CONTROLLING MEN'S SEX LIVES AT COLLEGE

The consequences for a wrongly convicted student are
devastating: Not only is he likely to be expelled, but he
may well be barred from graduate or professional school and
certain government agencies, suffer irreparable damage to
his reputation, and still be exposed to criminal prosecution.

—Peter Berkowitz in the *Wall Street Journal* discussing the
curtailing of due process rights for men on campus by
the Obama Administration[32]

Men are now subject to so many sexual harassment and
campus policies surrounding their sexuality that they
are afraid to have much to do with the multitudes of
women surrounding them on the average college campus. Women may complain that there are no men available, but, while there is a man shortage, the men who are
on campus are often reluctant to get involved with their
female cohorts because they lack the rights afforded to
a common criminal in a court of law. Of course, there
is the infamous 2006 Duke University case, where three
young men on the lacrosse team were falsely accused of
rape by a stripper named Crystal Mangum, and again
by the Duke professors and much of the community.[33]

It seemed like just the simple fact of being male was
enough to convict these young men even before a trial
or any hard evidence was brought forth. I even heard a
colleague say during the case that "all men in sports are
guilty." Just by virtue of being male, there is a presump-

tion of guilt in today's bastions of academic freedom. But there are many other lesser publicized discriminatory practices than the Duke case that also make being a man on campus detrimental to one's health and liberty, even for those not on a sports team.

Since the Duke case, you would think that colleges would have learned their lesson and seen the error of rushing to judge young men without evidence, but no such luck. If anything, it seems to have gotten worse. Many colleges, and now the Obama administration, have continued going after men and their sexuality in full force— guilty or not. According to the *Wall Street Journal*:

> Our universities impair liberal education not only by what they teach and do not teach in classrooms, but also by the illiberal rules they promulgate to regulate speech and conduct outside of class.
>
> The Obama administration has aggravated the problem. On April 4, Assistant Secretary for Civil Rights Russlynn Ali, head of the Department of Education's Office for Civil Rights (OCR), distributed a 19-page "Dear Colleague" letter to "provide recipients with information to assist them in meeting their obligations."
>
> At the cost of losing federal funding—on which all major institutions of higher education have grown dependent—colleges and universities are obliged under Title IX of the Civil Rights Act (which prohib-

its discrimination on the basis of sex) to thoroughly investigate all allegations of sexual harassment and sexual assault on campus, including the felony of rape. They are also obliged, according to Ms. Ali, to curtail due process rights of the accused.

OCR's new interpretation of Title IX "strongly discourages" universities from permitting the accused "to question or cross-examine the accuser" during the hearing. In addition, if universities provide an appeals process, it must be available to both parties—which subjects the accused to double jeopardy.[34]

In an article in the *Chronicle of Higher Education*, Sommers elaborates:

Deans at institutions including Yale, Stanford, and Brandeis Universities and the Universities of Georgia and of Oklahoma are already rushing to change their disciplinary procedures to meet the Education Department's decree. Now, on campuses throughout the country, we face the prospect of academic committees—armed with vague definitions of sexual assault, low standards of proof, and official sanction for the notion that sex under the influence is, ipso facto assault or rape—deciding the fate of students accused of a serious crime.

The new regulations should be seen for what they really are. They are not enlightened new procedures for protecting students from crime. They are a declaration of martial law against men, justified by an imaginary emergency, and a betrayal of the Title IX equity law.[35]

Many of these regulations are said to be needed because rape is "increasing" at the nation's colleges. However, much of this increase is the way that rape or sexual assaults are categorized.

The study cited by Ali used an online survey, conducted under a grant from the Justice Department, in which college women were asked about their sexual experiences, on campus and off, and the researchers—not the women themselves—decided whether they had been assaulted. The researchers employed an expansive definition of sexual assault that included "forced kissing" and even "attempted" forced kissing. The survey also asked subjects if they had sexual contact with someone when they were unable to give consent because they were drunk. A "yes" answer was automatically counted as a rape or assault. According to the authors, "an intoxicated person cannot legally consent to sexual contact."[36]

So only men can consent to sex when intoxicated? If he has sex when drunk, he is responsible, but if a woman does, she isn't? Isn't that sexist toward women? But as you can see, women are always seen as weak and vulnerable when it comes to consent to sex and men are always seen as the perpetrators—even if they are only fifteen years old, like in the last chapter where a young boy was ordered by the courts to pay for his thirty-four-year-old victimizer's baby. Teenage boys are apparently wise beyond their years when it comes to sex, but grown women must be protected from any sexual decisions they make when a man or boy is involved.

What this all really boils down to, however, is control over men's sexuality and freedom. The crackdown on fraternities, sports teams, and just everyday college guys by women's groups and the government is a way to keep men on guard and worrying that they will be charged with rape or sexual assault. After all, these organizations don't want men having too much fun, and if they do, they will get no due process and will be presumed guilty with little evidence. It's also about revenge against men for discrimination against women in the past. And it's okay with these groups even if innocent men pay the price.

A blogger who goes by the name Futurist said, "misandry (hatred of men) is the new Jim Crow."[37] Given some of these government and college regulations on men's sexuality, it seems to be heading in that direction in a milder form. Of course men should be held accountable if they *actually do* rape or sexually assault a woman, but to presume that men are guilty just because they are men and to need so little in the way of evidence to presume guilt is un-American where justice is supposed to be blind. Now it seems the new slogan is "justice is blind—unless the defendant is a man or boy."

Colleges have now become privileged finishing schools for girls. Except rather than teaching manners, they teach women that men are the enemy and men are treated as such on campus, unless they go along with the program that keeps them cowed or striking a PC pose. Many men have just decided that they don't belong in college and are going on strike, consciously or unconsciously. How will this affect their wages and lifestyles in the coming decades? If nothing changes and more and more men drop out of college or never attend, how will this change society? Will men continue to become the other, and be further relegated to second-class status where women and society are afraid of them and they are hesitant to participate fully in the public sphere? Is this already happening? The next chapter explores these questions.

CHAPTER 4

Why Does Dad Stay in the Basement?

PERVERTS, PREDATORS AND GOOFBALLS, OH MY!

> *Deeply embedded in my unconscious was the notion that all men*
> *are potential predators. That there is something inherently creepy*
> *to being born male. Logically, I don't buy this. Painting all men*
> *as potential predators makes guys feel bad about being guys and*
> *ladies feel distrustful. It's an unfair thought that reinforces bad*
> *behavior. I know I wouldn't feel good if half of the population*
> *were constantly eyeing me sideways. But as long as I had a*
> *female therapist and a lady adjusting my warrior pose,*
> *it was easy not to think too much about it.*
>
> —Rachel Rabbit White at *The Frisky* blog,
>   talking about why she is afraid of men[1]

Unfortunately many women, like White above, are afraid of men. This fear and even outright loathing of men has worked its way into the public realm and men are often looked at by society as perverts, possible predators and, at best, bumbling goofball dads relegated to the basement where they can't cause too much trouble. How did this happen? Why did men let it happen? These are good questions, and, as this chapter unfolds, I will attempt to answer them.

95

According to Kathleen Parker, author of *Save the Males*, "historians aren't sure of the precise date, but sometime around 1970, everyone in the United States drank acid-laced Kool-Aid, tie-dyed their brains, and decided fathers were no longer necessary."[2] Not only have many Western societies decided fathers aren't necessary, they have decided that most men are perverts, predators or goofballs who should be monitored in public and private spheres. So widespread is the problem of men being viewed as predators that a man can't even sit on an airline anymore without potentially being called out as a pervert:

> A businessman is suing British Airways over a policy that bans male passengers from sitting next to children they don't know—even if the child's parents are on the same flight.
>
> Mirko Fischer has accused the airline of branding all men as potential sex offenders and says innocent travelers are being publicly humiliated.
>
> In line with the policy, BA cabin crew patrol the aisles before take-off checking that youngsters traveling on their own or in a different row from their parents are not next to a male stranger.
>
> If they find a man next to a child or teenager they will ask him to move to a different seat. The aircraft will not take off unless the passenger obeys. . . .
>
> Mr. Fischer, who lives in Luxembourg with his

wife and their daughter Sophia, said: "This policy is branding all men as perverts for no reason. The policy and the treatment of male passengers is absolutely outrageous."

"A plane is a public place—cabin crew regularly walk down the aisles and passengers are sat so close to each other. The risk of any abuse is virtually zero."[3]

Good for Fischer for going after British Airways and making them sorry that they treated him and his fellow men as a bunch of perverts, but this should never have been allowed to happen in the first place. And surely he isn't the first guy this has happened to. What about the others? Did they just passively move their seat to another in the back of the plane? Perhaps you think this is not that big of a deal. Who wants to sit next to a kid anyway? However, the idea that companies and the public can so easily discriminate against men on a major airline is troubling, to say the least.

The culture is full of these negative stereotypes about men, and people toss them around without a care, kind of like White in the quote at the beginning of this chapter. White may think she is keeping her thoughts of men in her subconscious, but this distrust comes out in ways that permeate the culture and affect men's behavior. If people are afraid or upset about something to do with women, they keep it to themselves. Men are fair game and the stakes are high: One wrong move and a man could be looking at jail time or being placed on a sex offender registry.

However, the cost to society of portraying men in this manner is high. Because men are afraid to engage in many areas of public life and work, especially those that involve children, kids have fewer and fewer role models and can end up harmed or worse, dead. "A poll conducted by a NCH, a children's charity, and volunteer group Chance UK, has identified what they believe is the reason so many charities are struggling to recruit men to work with children. Turns out, many men are afraid of being labeled as pedophiles."[4]

Two-year-old Abigail Rae died by drowning in a village pond in England. Her death stirred a debate because "the ongoing inquest revealed an explosive fact. A man passing by was afraid to guide the lost child to safety because he feared being labeled 'a pervert.'"[5]

The man's name was Clive Peachey, and his actions were the topic of a lively debate. Though it is terrible, can you really blame him for walking away? Some people did, mostly women, but they should try living in a man's shoes for a while and they also might go on strike where interactions with minors are concerned. As author Wendy McElroy said about this case, "child abuse must be addressed but it is worse than folly to punish those who help children. Our society is creating Clive Peachey—decent men who will walk away from a child in need. Abby Rae died not only from drowning but also from bad politics."[6]

These high-profile cases cause other men to avoid children who aren't their own for fear that they will be accused of who knows what. But there are times when a man is just out in his car minding his own business when he comes head to head with a minor, even though he didn't mean to do so. Wendy McElroy explains:

Last summer, an Illinois man lost an appeal on his conviction as a sex offender for grabbing the arm of a 14-year-old girl. She had stepped directly in front of his car, causing him to swerve in order to avoid hitting her.

The 28-year-old Fitzroy Barnaby jumped out his car, grabbed her arm and lectured her on how not to get killed. Nothing more occurred. Nevertheless, that one action made him guilty of "the unlawful restraint of a minor," which is a sexual offense in Illinois. Both the jury and judge believed him. Nevertheless, Barnaby went through years of legal proceedings that ended with his name on a sex offender registry, where his photograph and address are publicly available. He must report to authorities. His employment options are severely limited; he cannot live near schools or parks.[7]

I was once in California many years ago as a teenager and was riding a bike on a sidewalk on a busy road and fell in front of a car. The man in the car almost hit me and his adrenaline was high. He did the same thing as

Barnaby; he grabbed my arm and yelled at me to be more careful. He was visibly shaken and was probably just upset that he had been placed in a position where he could have killed me. I was grateful for the warning and didn't ride a bike on such a busy street again. The guy did me a favor. Now a guy like that is taken to court and charged as a sex offender. It's more than pathetic; it should be criminal.

When men hear about cases like this, they understandably react with fear and withdrawal. This is not really a strike, per se, but more of a reluctant retreat. At a parent's site called Parent Dish, men shared their feelings of vulnerability when it came to interacting with kids.[8]

Iggy writes in:
I as a male am afraid to be around little children, I have one on the way, but up until now I have been without kids and I will be 31 this year. Just recently at a family function on my wife's side, her stepmom invited some of her family to the function and I was SHOCKED when one of the little girls that had been clinging to me all day came up to me and said "My mom said I can't play with you any more cause she doesn't know what you'll do to me." I took this very hard because for one, I love kids, and for some reason they love me. I am a volunteer firefighter and always the first one to sign up to do safety talks with the kids and just this one instance set me back a TON. . . .[9]

NV wrote in to the Parent Dish:

I used to coach girls' soccer with my fiancée (now wife). I stopped because one of the girls (all of 8 years old) said:

"I don't have to listen to you. I can get you in trouble just by telling people you touched me."

Now that I have a child of my own, I have no idea how I'm going to be involved when he wants to do sports or other activities.

I already got odd looks on the playground the year I was a stay-at-home dad and carting him around with me all the time.[10]

And it's no wonder that kids and their parents—though adults should know better—think that men are dangerous; the media portrays men as villains who abduct kids or are pedophiles or perverts. Unfortunately, women's groups are all atwitter about women being portrayed in the media as having to be beautiful or interested in beauty, but it is much worse to be shown as a suspicious pervert who should be lynched or locked up by society.

It makes people suspicious of the average man, and the threat of jail is held over his head for making the wrong move such as helping a child. Women who are indoctrinated to use too many beauty products may just lose a few bucks to vanity. Yet, guess which sex has advocates railing against the media for their portrayal of women? Documentaries like *Miss Representation* are shown to school children to teach girls about how they are negatively portrayed in the media and how to deal with negative stereotypes. Boys are offered no such education. If they are, it is to tell them what a bunch of sexists they are and how they can change to accommodate girls and women.

A male reader emailed to let me know about his experience with his daughter's school. Bobby is the father of a high school girl and he received a letter from the head of his daughter's school telling him that "the student body, faculty, and staff will come together to watch Jennifer Siebel Newsom's documentary, *Miss Representation*." Once Bobby read up on the film, he was afraid that his daughter was essentially going to be brainwashed by the school to feel like a victim via a film telling girls they were devalued and powerless while boys had the world at their feet. It's no wonder that so many girls feel angry after seeing all the propaganda thrown at them by our schools and culture.

The school sent links to the parents to let them know about the film and discussed what an empowering opportunity this would be for the girls in the class. I looked at one of the links in which the filmmaker— who is the wife of Gavin Newsom, the lieutenant governor of California—was in a video describing how our culture devalued little girls and told boys the world was their oyster. She was upset that when her son was born,

he received little shirts and bibs saying "future president" and her daughter did not receive one.[11] Apparently, Newsom tearfully concluded that boys were on
easy street and girls got the shaft by society and the
media. The film is described as follows:

> The film *Miss Representation* exposes how American
> youth are being sold the concept that women and
> girls' value lies in their youth, beauty and sexuality.
> It's time to break that cycle of mistruths.
>
> In response we created MissRepresentation.org,
> a call-to-action campaign that seeks to empower
> women and girls to challenge limiting media labels
> in order to realize their potential.
>
> We are uniting individuals around a common,
> meaningful goal to spark millions of small actions
> that ultimately lead to a cross-generational move-
> ment to eradicate gender stereotypes and create last-
> ing cultural and sociological change.[12]

It's fine that this woman made such a film, but my concern is the following:

> Schools are using the *Miss Representation*'s curriculum
> to educate youth around media literacy and to inspire
> and activate students to make change. Communities
> are hosting screenings and discussions to shift the
> cultural mindset around gender and end sexism.[13]

Why are schools playing such propaganda in the classroom and doing so without showing how boys and men
are equally discriminated against? Bobby, the father of
the high school girl, wrote to the head of the school and
let her know that he wanted alternative views to this film
discussed and other information about how boys and men
are treated in the media presented, but no such luck. The
head of the school insisted that the film was just fine as it
was and that it was so very important to have conversa-
tions about girls. No mention of how boys were treated.
She offered to send the film to Bobby, and he took her up
on the offer and watched the film. This was his reply to
me and to the head of the school about the film:

> Hi Helen:
> The Head of School did send me a copy of *Miss Rep-
> resentation*. The movie was more outlandish than I
> expected (see copy of email below for my comments
> to her). Katie Couric in the movie (rough quote): "If
> women were in charge, we would solve all the world's
> problems in months."
>
> My email to Head of School: —Bobby
>
> Dear Ms. Head of School:
> Thanks for sending your copy of *Miss Representation*.
> I plan to return the copy in the next few days after I
> view the teaching material.

I have viewed the movie and consider it just another cliché of women as victims. I suggest again that
you access the links I sent to find alternative perspec-
tives that do not degrade women.

You'll find below the "glam pic" of Ms. Newsom
from her website, indicating that she has yet to overcome the need to fulfill the role she spent an entire
movie castigating.[14]

"Well played, Bobby," I thought when I read the letter.
Luckily for Bobby, his daughter was too wise to fall for
the indoctrination and there was some discussion in her
class that boys were also portrayed negatively by the
media. Dear Reader, you will probably be glad to know
that the filmmaker, Newsom, said that her next project
will be on boys, and I can only imagine what that documentary will be like—probably some diatribe about how
boys need to break free of gender stereotypes, become
even more emasculated and help girls succeed more than
they already have. If boys become much more "powerful," they will probably make up only 30 percent of college students, instead of slightly more than 40 percent.

What truly bothers me about "noble" souls like Newsom is that they refuse to look at reality. A few men are
in positions of power and many more are in the middle
or at the bottom of society. Women tend to congregate
more toward the middle. I wonder, if women had the
choice, whether they would really make the trade with

men and have a few women at the top, and many more women at the bottom. I kind of doubt it. But with documentaries like *Miss Representation* and the subsequent indoctrination in the schools, the focus is always on girls and how they are a bunch of victims. The boys are left to fend for themselves or told that they are the cause of the world's ills.

But the negative stereotype of men as predators and perverts is actually a very real concern for young boys who often are not around any real live men. According to the U.S. Census Bureau, 24 million boys are raised in fatherless homes.[15] Male teachers in elementary schools are rare; they account for only 16 percent of all elementary school teachers.[16] Dr. Jim Macnamara is an Australian professor of public communications in Sydney who analyzed two thousand mass media portrayals of men and male identity and found that men were depicted mostly as villains, aggressors, perverts and philanderers.[17] He also found that "by volume, 69 percent of mass media reporting and commentary on men was unfavorable, compared with just 12 percent favorable and 19 percent neutral or balanced."[18]

"Highly negative views of men and male identity provide little by way of positive role models for boys to find out what it means to be a man and gives boys little basis for self-esteem," said Macnamara. "In the current environment where there is an identified lack of positive role models in the physical world . . . the lack of positive role models in the media and presence of overwhelmingly negative images should be of concern. . . . Ultimately such portrayals could lead to negative social and even financial cost for society in areas such as male health, rising suicide rates and family disintegration."[19]

Sadly, the only men on television these days who are not portrayed negatively are metrosexuals, according to Macnamara.[20] Maybe feminized men are the only men women like Ms. White, the woman who was afraid of men at the beginning of the chapter, feel comfortable around. And we all know that nothing in our society is more important than making women feel comfortable and with high self-esteem to boot.

Kathleen Parker has an excellent section in her book *Save the Males* on how men are basically portrayed as goofballs and idiots. She correctly asks about children, "What message are they absorbing today when nearly every TV father is absent or absurd? Or when children are always smarter than the old man?"[21] However, with this interpretation, she misses the boat: "Over time, negative stereotyping is absorbed into the culture, and the message is that men are not only bad, they're stupid and unreliable. . . . All things considered, male bashing is probably not a terrible threat to civilization."[22] Parker's latter analysis is that male bashing is not all that bad but that it leads to boy bashing, which is bad.

I would argue that both are bad and that male bashing *is* a threat to civilization. I think that many men would agree with me. I asked men in a blog post at PJ Media to discuss negative images of men in the media and received more than 240 responses. Here are some of the highlights.[23]

Richard Ricardo says:
Watch any modern (1990's +) cartoon and you will get the same messages about males/men: that they are inferior to women. It is part of an overall plot to weaken our society. Schools ingrain this same philosophy/message all day long, and on the weekends and after school, the television finishes the job.[24]

Tex Taylor states:
What faster way to reshape civilization in the mold of progressivism than to minimize the male role, make them the weaker sex and feminize the boys?[25]

Mac says:
Yes, the incessant male bashing is disgusting and hateful. However, if women are stupid enough to fall for it, they deserve what they get. What lots of them aren't getting is married, and a lot of that is because more and more men are seeing the truth about women's part in the society surrounding us. . . .

Long story short, women have much more to fear in a world where men not only don't respect them but actually dislike them. It's coming to that, and the women have only themselves to blame. Young girls today are going to live in a much harder world because of the choices their mothers and sisters made in the last 30 years.[26]

Bob says:

I have been saying for 15+ years now that TV shows and commercials portray men as idiots, morons, objects of ridicule and humiliation, etc. . . . I'm on strike and have been for years now. Women are so full of hatred and disdain for me, and they have been bred with this idea that they are "empowered" to rule over us in every way. Family law has done the same; completely stacked against men and gives women total power over relationships and family. It simply doesn't make sense anymore to connect with women on a long term basis; and forget about marriage. With feminism inculcating the idea that women should rule and dominate men (by trashing them in ads and shows, and elsewhere), it is an absolute danger for a man to get married. The modern American woman does not make for a secure relationship; it is fraught with nothing but risk and you are basically walking on eggshells throughout it all. There is just way too much emotional, psychological, financial, and gender risk at stake for the man. Women are infused with a sense of power over men and entitlement that should not exist. If you go against the feminist ideas with which they have been bred, you are simply dead in the water . . . and you become nothing more than a proof point for all the negative things feminism taught them.

Also, why would you want to get married and have children? Would you want your son or daughter to learn that all men are objects of derision, ridicule, humiliation? That they are fat, bumbling, stupid, idiotic jerks? That women are the strong, smart, visionary, logical, problem solving, sensible, good natured, great looking, healthy ones? That's what they will learn, plain and simple. Even if there's a pre-nup regarding the assets, the other risks are just too great for a guy since money is only one aspect of a relationship that can go bad.

I foresee a nation of primarily single people by the latter half of the century, driven by the feminist movement and the obsessive focus to "empower" women over men.[27]

As these male readers have mentioned, male bashing leads to generalized hostility against men, which in turn harms society. So yes, Ms. Parker, male bashing is a terrible threat to civilization. Subsequent laws and cultural norms that stem from male bashing lead to issues touched on in the next section that looks at how our society is controlling men by controlling their space. For it is male bashing and the resultant hostility and resentment of men that is sending Dad to the basement just to carve out a place where he can get some peace. With Dad hiding out and afraid to make waves, civilization may never be the same.

THE DECLINE OF MALE SPACE

> *Fantastic topic. There was no sadder scene to a movie than in "Juno" when married guy Jason Bateman realized that in his entire huge house, he had only a large closet to keep all the stuff he loved. That hit me like a punch in the face.*
>
> —Commenter Playstead at *The Art of Manliness* website in response to "The Decline of Male Space"[28]

Do you ever go around and wonder where all the men have gone? It seems as though women have taken over much of the public space (except perhaps for sports events) and they even seem now like the masters of the home, too. If you watch shows like HGTV's *House Hunters*, you will notice the theme is often that the women act like the house is their domain exclusively: The wife excitedly exclaims how big the closet is and asks the husband "where will you keep your stuff?" as an afterthought. Sure, this is probably just banter for the show to make it look "cute," but it's annoying and indicative of the lack of space that men are allowed in their own homes.

And what about in the public sphere? It seems that

men are no longer getting together as often. Remember when men went to bars after work, went to the Elks club, or the Freemasons, and hung out and talked together? When was the last time you or your friends did this (especially if you are over forty)? I remember once a male acquaintance was shocked because my husband had the day off to just go out, be with friends or enjoy a hobby while I watched our child. Apparently, if a man with a family is free to go out and have a good time, it's news.

Brett McKay, the author (along with his wife, Kate) of *The Art of Manliness* books, wrote a terrific piece on the web called "The Decline of Male Space," in which he argues that while we have made progress in integrating the workplace and home, which is good, "the pendulum has arguably swung too far to the other extreme, leaving men without their own space."[29] Suburban living gave rise to more of a focus on family life, and women were more and more in charge of family life:

> The period after WWII was filled with dramatic changes in American life. One of the most powerful changes was the migration of white, middle class families from cities to the suburbs. Large developments like Levittown provided returning vets a chance to buy a piece of the American Dream for a relatively affordable price and get started on raising a family.
>
> The rise of suburban culture with its emphasis on creating a domestic nest, usually meant sacrificing

male space for the good of the family. Home designs in the 1950s exchanged the numerous, smaller rooms of the Victorian home for fewer, larger rooms. The goal was to create more open space where families could congregate together and bond while watching the *Honeymooners* on TV.

With no room to call their own, men were forced to build their male sanctuaries in the most uninhabitable parts of a home. Garages, attics, and basements quickly became the designated space for men, while the women and children had free reign [*sic*] over the rest of the house.[30]

It is not just suburban living that has given rise to the decline of male space; it is also the pressure from women's groups, society and the government:

In addition to fraternal lodges, male only clubs and restaurants served as a place where a man could enjoy a nice rib-eye with their bros and get candid advice on their career and family life. But male-only clubs would start to feel the squeeze when the U.S. Supreme Court held in 1987 that states and cities may constitutionally ban sex discrimination by business-oriented private clubs. With this green light from the Court, many states and cities started cracking down on male-only clubs and restaurants. New York City was especially vigorous in prosecuting male-only clubs. Perhaps the most famous instance of a once male-only club being forced to open membership to women was the New York Athletic Club. Founded in 1868, the club contained dining rooms, bars, an indoor pool, and a block long gym. Facing legal pressure, the New York Athletic Club opened its membership to women in 1989 with mixed feelings on the part of members. Despite the legal and societal pressure, a few-male only clubs still exist in the U.S.[31]

While I applaud women being able to join and use public facilities and private ones within reason, it seems that we have crossed a line in our society where men are actually being singled out and isolated from each other by the government and the society. With this crackdown in 1987 and well before, our culture has steadily made it almost obscene for men to congregate on their own together. It seems that people are afraid for groups of men to get together because they might decide that they don't like what's going on in the culture today and actually do something about it. Men's space is now being controlled for political reasons.

Women and their minions want men isolated so they won't band together politically, and it keeps men under women's thumb in the domestic realm. If a man does something at home that a woman doesn't like, he's one step away from the police or social services stepping in with a restraining order or worse, taking his kids. Or he is afraid of being kicked out of his own house. I once knew a man who was a detective who was frightened of his wife who kept tabs on him and didn't want him around friends and family. When I asked him why he put up with this abuse, he said that he lived in his family home and if he made any waves, he feared his wife could take half the property and this would disappoint his family. If he were a woman, there would be somewhere to turn for help. As a man, he slept on the couch and finally ended up with a heart condition that was exacerbated by stress. He felt he had no recourse than to deal with the situation alone. If he had had a lodge or male friends to turn to, he might have found some other solution that would have been easier on his health.

Charles Murray, in his book *Coming Apart: The State of White America, 1960–2010*, writes about the role of secular fraternal associations. "Today, most people know of organizations such as the Elks, Moose, and Odd Fellows (if they know them at all) as male lower-middle-class social clubs. They are actually the remnants of a mosaic of organizations that were a central feature of American civic life. . . . For our purposes, one is particularly salient: They drew their membership from across the social classes, and ensured regular, close interaction among people of different classes."[32]

As I think about these fraternal organizations, perhaps another important role they served was to get different classes of people talking and brainstorming about

ideas and problems. Because there were different social classes present, those men who had certain problems could talk them over with other men who might
be more successful problem solvers. If a businessman
needed help with something mechanical, he might find
a successful mechanic there who could tell him what to
do, and, vice versa, a mechanic might find a successful
businessman who could help him with money issues. Or
men could talk to other men across classes who were
more successful in resolving problems at home. Or men
could just congregate and discuss politics and how to
challenge threats to justice, liberty and freedom.

Now men are discouraged and actively made fun of or
denied the ability to be in all-male groups by the law and
by the disapproval of certain segments of the culture. For
example, look at how colleges treat fraternity guys; they
are all looked at with suspicion and treated like they are
one step away from gang-raping the next girl who walks
by their frat house. If you don't believe me, mention frat
guys and watch the reaction of any woman over the age
of about thirty. Most look at them with fear and disdain
and want a stop put to any fun they might be having. And
as men get older, the isolation and denigration get worse.
I wonder how much of the demonization of men leads to
our staggering male suicide rate? Men kill themselves at
much higher rates than women: four men for every one
woman. It's politically correct to laugh at men, beat them
or hurl insults their way. Most men don't say anything

and just retreat to the basement to tune out the world, and who can blame them?

A wounded animal retreats to its cave and now America's men are doing the same thing down in their "man caves." Yes, it's nice that men at least have some place in the house to call their own. However, the man cave is really no more than a booby prize for men who must swallow their manhood and head downstairs in order to get some peace and hope that the womenfolk and the government stay out of their way. In an article called "Why He Needs a Man Cave," the author—a woman— treats her husband more like a teen whom she is allowing to dress up a room in the house than an equal partner who probably paid for at least half the house. She has a number of little rules for women concerning the "construction" of the man cave, including:

> After you settle on a place, let him decorate it. Don't worry, men's taste with décor isn't as expensive as a women's [sic]. Guys like caves and can do with minimal stuff . . . usually. . . .
>
> I would never help build a man cave for my man if I didn't trust him. In fact, I wouldn't share a home with anyone I didn't trust. We aren't going to build a man cave this year, but I am going to help make "his space" at our home more comfortable. He wants a new desk for his computer. He chose one that didn't match the décor, but it is his man cave within our home.[33]

Wow, a whole desk in the house that a guy got to pick out, how egalitarian. This writer's husband would be lucky to get a basement. But even that seems kind of lame. Now men have no place to turn except the boob tube down in the basement, where they watch themselves being characterized as perverts, predators and goofballs. Add to that some Cheetos and a bunch of beer to kill the pain, and inertia sets in. Some men profess to be happy down there, but then, those who are wounded by others often don't see the obvious.

When a partner isolates their spouse from friends, associates, and public places, it's called domestic abuse. When it's done to an entire gender, it's called feminism. It is imperative to stop this abuse against men and allow saner laws and minds to prevail. The next chapter will look at the repercussions to society of the war on men; though it started long ago, at some point it will end in the suicide of our society as we know it unless we do something about it.

CHAPTER 5

Why It Matters

"Dude, where's my lifeboat?"
—Rich Lowry at *National Review*, explaining the new
attitude of men in the twenty-first century[1]

On January 13, 2012, an Italian cruise ship, the *Costa Concordia*, partially sank off the coast of Tuscany with 4,252 people on board; thirty people died, sixty-four were injured and a couple are still missing.[2] The captain, Francesco Schettino, was charged with "abandoning in-capacitated passengers and failing to inform maritime au-thorities."[3] Crew members were not much more help than the captain as passengers reported that many of them left passengers to fend for themselves. Rich Lowry at *National Review* compared the crash of the *Costa Concordia* to the *Titanic* and how men responded in each:

> "Every man for himself" is a phrase associated with the deadly *Costa Concordia* disaster, but not as a last-minute expedient. It appears to have been the natural order of things. In the words of one newspaper ac-count, "An Australian mother and her young daugh-ter have described being pushed aside by hysterical men as they tried to board lifeboats." If the men of the *Titanic* had lived to read such a thing, they would

have recoiled in shame. The *Titanic*'s crew surely would have thought the hysterics deserved to be shot on sight—and would have volunteered to perform the service.

Women and children were given priority in theory, but not necessarily in practice. The Australian mother said of the scene, "We just couldn't believe it—especially the men, they were worse than the women." Another woman passenger agreed, "There were big men, crew members, pushing their way past us to get into the lifeboats." Yet another, a grandmother, complained, "I was standing by the lifeboats and men, big men, were banging into me and knocking the girls."

Guys aboard the *Costa Concordia* apparently made sure the age of chivalry was good and dead by pushing it over and trampling on it in their heedless rush for the exits.[4]

Lowry seems to be blaming men for what happened on the *Concordia* by saying that the guys aboard made sure that chivalry is good and dead, but he misses the point. The guys' behavior is a culmination that has been years in the making. Our society, the media, the government, women, white knights and Uncle Tims have regulated and demanded that any incentives men have for acting like men be taken away and decried masculinity as evil. Now they are seeing the result. Men have been listening to what society has been saying about them for more than forty years; they are perverts, wimps, cowards, assholes, jerks, good-for-nothing, bumbling deadbeats and expendable. Men got the message; now they are acting accordingly. As you sow, so shall you reap.

So now people are surprised when men are heading for the exits? They shouldn't be surprised. Men have been pushed there for some time. We should actually be surprised that it has taken so long.

The *Concordia* is just a microcosm of what is happening in our greater society. Men are opting out, bailing out and going on strike in response to the attack on their gender; a society can't spend more than forty years tearing down almost half of the population and expect them to respond with "give me another" forever. Pretty soon, a lot more men will be taking Captain Schettino's lead and jumping ship—only it will be on a lot larger scale than a boatload of people. The war on men is suicidal for our society in so many ways, and treating men like the enemy is dangerous, both to men and to the society that needs their positive participation as fathers, husbands, role models and leaders.

Yes, we need women as role models and leaders, but that has been the theme for more than forty years, and girls and women have support in those areas and are doing well. More women than men are going to college,[5] the fastest-growing jobs are those primarily occupied by women[6] and women consume more health care dollars than men do.[7] Our society has been building women up for decades and tearing men down for the same amount of time, and they are not doing so well as a group. Women are empowered; men are assholes who might rape you. That message, as the next section describes, is not a good one in promoting a healthy society.

STEREOTYPING MEN MAKES FOR A BAD SOCIETY

> *But these stereotypes also poison our public discourse, distort our understanding of the real differences among us, and reduce the chances for resolving those differences even in part. These stereotypes corrode the bonds of mutual concern and respect that hold a pluralistic society together. . . . To corrode these bonds unnecessarily is a dangerous thing.*
>
> —Douglas Laycock, in "Vicious Stereotypes in Polite Society"[8]

In the late 1980s, Wendy Brown, a professor of women's studies, came face-to-face with a man who was culturally different from her while backpacking in the Sierra Nevada with friends. Her car had broken down, and she enlisted the help of a sportsman nearby who was wearing a National Rifle Association cap, drinking a beer, reading a porn magazine and scouting out the area for his hunting club. This kind man spent two hours helping this professor get her car started. You can probably guess the rest of the story. Naturally, for his trouble, Brown stereotyped him in an article in the *Yale Law Journal* as a potential rapist and had the audacity to exclaim, "During the hours I spent with him, I had no reason to conclude that his respect for women's personhood ran any deeper than his respect for the lives of the Sierra deer."[9]

Luckily, law professor Douglas Laycock wrote a rebuttal to Brown's piece, stating why Brown was wrong for stereotyping a man who gave two hours of his time to help her—a woman after all! But his point is bigger than just two strangers meeting in the woods. He extrapolates from Brown's anecdote to the larger society:

> But these stereotypes also poison our public discourse, distort our understanding of the real differences among us, and reduce the chances for resolving those differences even in part. These stereotypes corrode the bonds of mutual concern and respect that hold a pluralistic society together. These bonds are stretched enough by honest disagreement and simple demands for change. Once in our history they broke entirely, and some minority groups have been placed outside their protection for long periods. But generally these bonds have held. They make it unsurprising when Americans from "opposite ends of the political and cultural universe" help one another.
>
> To corrode these bonds unnecessarily is a dangerous thing. And we should have no illusions about

who is most endangered. In any outbreak of intolerance, in any reduction of mutual concern and respect, the weak and oppressed will suffer more than the strong and dominant. Those who are most endangered by stereotypes and prejudice have special reasons to avoid invoking their own stereotypes and prejudices against others.[10]

As Laycock indicates, our society is built with the implicit understanding that, although we are all different, there are commonalities as Americans that bind us, and with that bond comes a willingness to help each other. What happens when those bonds erode and we are left without a lifeboat, kind of like what happened on the *Concordia* to some of the passengers who didn't make it out alive? If we continue to teach men and boys that it is "every man for himself" by stereotyping, isolating and penalizing them for the crime of being born male in the twenty-first century, they will be reluctant to help or interact with women or others who may possibly endanger them. Our culture then comes to have a more dog-eat-dog quality that may limit our survival. People—both men and women—don't know who they can trust, and society can break down to a third-world level.

Warren Farrell was interviewed for *Forbes* and made an important point that addresses why we need to focus on men's issues in terms of their benefits to society:

Virtually every society that survived did so by so-cializing its sons to be disposable. Disposable in war; disposable in work. We need warriors and volunteer firefighters so we label these men heroes. Men need the approval, and want to be eligible for marriage and fatherhood, so we all have a vested interest in not questioning this socialization for disposability. Thus, men don't speak up and women don't hear what men don't say. But exactly because men's attitude toward their own problems remains "when the going gets tough, the tough get going," and because few men realize that their facade of strength is their weakness, this outreach to the silent sex is all the more important.[11]

Farrell's observation underscores two important points. The first is that society *needs* strong, capable men to do the things that it can't do without and that, frankly, few women are really willing or able to do. The second is that by socializing men to serve in those roles, it has also socialized them out of being able to speak up when they are mistreated or taken for granted. Perhaps those Italian seamen were better complainers than the aver-age American man—but do we really want to live in a women-and-children-last world? I don't think that many men would really be happy with that either. A better so-lution is for men to retain their male virtues but learn to speak up for themselves when needed. Society—or at least the parts of society that cater to women—may not like that, but it's a change society needs to make.

WHY MEN OPTING OUT ISN'T GOOD FOR SOCIETY

> *Men slowly discover that the effort to win women's attention via employment is not rewarding them the way it did for their dads and granddads, and that now only herculean efforts to make considerably more than women will give them an edge in the mating market.*
> —Blogger Chateau Heartiste, on why men are opting out[12]

Men are now opting out of work and marriage altogether or are just not trying as hard in many cases. While this may be good for individual men, it is not good for society as a whole. The system we now have in place treats men with little to no respect and does not reward them but actively punishes them for doing the things that society has come to expect. Women as a whole don't seem to like that men are now going on strike. For example, Lisa Belkin, a senior columnist at the *Huffington Post*, wrote an article entitled "Why Men Opting-Out Should Make You Angry," suggesting that, yes, women should be angry that men have decided to opt out:

> I have always wondered whether there would be the same anger at a story about men choosing to ratchet

back their careers—work less, earn less, climb less of the ladder. . . .

Liza Mundy's new book, "The Richer Sex: How the New Majority of Female Breadwinners is Transforming Sex, Love and Family," is about many things. As its title suggests, it starts with the prediction that the economic relationship between the sexes is about to flip. Women are already outpacing men in some places and professions, Mundy writes, and in a shift that she compares to "the rise of agrarian society, the dawn of the industrial age, the ascent of the white-collar office worker, and the opening of the global economy" she extrapolates that women will come to be the majority of primary breadwinners in the US. . . .

There's a lot to process—it takes Mundy an entire book—so let's start with the section titled "The Opt-Out Revolution—Among Men." Yes, it's apparently their turn. Back in 1970, she writes, 80 percent of working age men were employed full-time, a number that has dropped over the decades to only 66 percent. Some of the reasons are cause for despair: unemployment, incarceration. But one segment have left the workplace for reasons Mundy celebrates— educated men who describe themselves as less ambitious, less likely to believe that men should earn more than women, and more interested in spending time with their children, and increasingly aware that the workplace, as constructed, makes it much too hard to do it all. . . .

Amy Vachon is the author, with her husband Marc, of the book "Equally Shared Parenting: Rewriting The Rules For A New Generation Of Parents." They, too, thought that the future would look different than this—one that looks like their own carefully crafted life, where both men and women find work that is fulfilling (but does not take 70 hours a week) and are reasonably well paid (though not enough to necessarily support a family without a second income) and both partners share equally in chores and child rearing, but also get time for themselves.

Substituting one kind of inequity for another we mean we have travelled far and gotten nowhere, they warn. "If we flip the power to women, we'll just end up with the same role responsibility burdens and imbalanced lives," Amy told me, only with the genders reversed.[13]

"Welcome to reality, Ms. Belkin," I thought. I enjoyed reading the comments to her article, which pretty much pointed out the same thing—that men have been dealing with a difficult situation for quite some time:

Rudy in la asks:
Have men opted out or been kicked out? There's a difference and I wonder which one is causing this "phenomenon."[14]

Afkbrad says:

Men are going Galt these days and it is a well deserved thing. It is time the ladies worked 70–80 hours a week while the ladies support us for a few generations. They can die early and give men half during a divorce. While we are at it, I firmly believe women need to get some skin in the game during wars. America's sons shouldn't be the only ones good enough to be sent into the meat grinder of combat. A few million of our daughters need a military funeral so there's some parity. You ladies can have the stress while we kick back so you can support us for a change.[15]

Whether men were kicked out or opted out of the job market and marriage, we should all be concerned with where this is leading as a society. Let me say again that as an individual man, opting out or going on strike is a valuable tool that may serve you well. I will even discuss it as an option in the next chapter on fighting back. However, for a society, it is detrimental to have so many men, especially young men, no longer willing, or unable to participate fully in work and in marriage. Charles Murray, in an article for the *Wall Street Journal*, points out that blue-collar men have been opting out of jobs and marriage even when the economy was good. He explains why:

If changes in the labor market don't explain the development of the new lower class, what does? My own explanation is no secret. In my 1984 book "Losing Ground," I put the blame on our growing welfare state and the perverse incentives that it created. I also have argued that the increasing economic independence of women, who flooded into the labor market in the 1970s and 1980s, played an important role.

Simplifying somewhat, here's my reading of the relevant causes: Whether because of support from the state or earned income, women became much better able to support a child without a husband over the period of 1960 to 2010. As women needed men less, the social status that working-class men enjoyed if they supported families began to disappear. The sexual revolution exacerbated the situation, making it easy for men to get sex without bothering to get married. In such circumstances, it is not surprising that male fecklessness bloomed, especially in the working class.[16]

Naturally, white-knight Murray's solution is to shame men into doing the "right thing," but how much more shaming can society do? Short of locking up men for not marrying and working their fingers to the bone for women and kids, they are shaming men already. Anyone heard the word "man-child" that gets tossed around in books, magazines and the media like candy? An insightful blogger who calls himself Chateau Heartiste describes why these men are actually opting out:

Men, like men always do, are simply reacting to the conditions set on the ground by women.

Murray sees this, but doesn't run with it. Women's improved employment numbers, education and earning power (some of it contributed by government largesse) has had the effect of SHRINKING their acceptable dating pool. Material resources and occupational status are one way women judge men's mate worthiness (not the only way, but the one way that viscerally matters to most beta males), and the innate female sexual disposition to be attracted— ANIMALISTICALLY ATTRACTED—to men with higher status and more resources than themselves necessarily means that financially independent women and government-assisted women are going to find fewer men in their social milieu attractive.

Result? Men slowly discover that the effort to win women's attention via employment is not rewarding them the way it did for their dads and granddads, and that now only herculean efforts to make considerably more than women will give them an edge in the mating market. The male fecklessness that Murray lambasts is actually a rational male response to a changing sexual market where the rewards of female sexuality go disproportionately to charming, aloof jerks over meager beta providers.[17]

This lack of enthusiasm for work is showing up in the workforce statistics. The *Daily Mail*, a British newspaper, pointed out a staggering statistic in a recent column: "The 69.9 percent labor force participation rate for men is at lowest level ever recorded."[18] I was so surprised at this low number that I wrote a blog post asking my readers: "Why is the participation rate of men in the workforce so low?"[19] Here is what they said.

JKB says:

Why work? Once you've made your nut, why do more? The 'profits' are eaten up either by your dependents, which is good, or now by the government, which is bad. Are the men completely out of the workforce or are they just not consistent? Or have white males just found alternative ways to keep themselves up than to participate by continual effort in a game rigged to favor others? I don't think that so many men have dropped out completely but they sure might have dropped out of the government statistics created to track a large industrial workforce that stayed under the thumb of an employer or union.[20]

Oso Pardo states:

Personally, I've not dropped out of the traditional workforce, but am getting very close to that decision. The kids are out of college and employed, the wife is semi-retired and I'm getting really close to saying "screw it" and going back to consulting (I'm an Engineer) only this time for small jobs and cash only. The "safety net" looks to have become a nice comfortable hammock. Why continue to work my brains out only to support others who look down on me with disdain?[21]

Vic states:

Men are doing the math. When you see your friends vilified in family court by their "Christian" wives, you have to take a step back and ask yourself a question. If that admired pastor with 30 years of ministry, community service and business is going to lose his kids, income and ministry because his wife isn't happy anymore, what chance do I have?[22]

Finally, commenter tobytylersf states:

I work in a law firm, in a staff position. I haven't had a man for a boss in over 17 years. That is normal in most offices, as most middle-management positions are now filled by women. Since most people hiring hire people who look like themselves, guess what? Women managers tend to hire more women. It's that simple, I think. Regardless of whatever "war on women" the Democrats claim, women still control most of the wealth in this country, and, since they are most of the middle managers in corporations, they control most of the hiring. Go figure.[23]

Men are both being forced out and dropping out of the workforce in spades and our society doesn't care unless women like Lisa Belkin use the fact to complain about how it affects women. Maybe when there are no more men working, people will start to notice, until then, they will just continue to discuss the "war on women" until there are no men anywhere. Maybe that is what the feminists wanted all along. One thing is clear, if women were dropping out of the workforce at this rate, it would be considered a national crisis. But if men do it, there is hardly a whimper. But then, perhaps, that is how the society will go down, not with a bang, but with a whimper, because no one is listening.

It seems that the task of living up to women's expectations is so high that many men just don't measure up. They simply give up and find a life that brings them some reasonable amount of comfort. Yes, the basement, video games and porn might be a poor second (or not), but at least it's attainable and doesn't sit around trying to shame them for not performing up to par. The problem for society is that even good women—who like men and would be glad to have a husband or partner—often lose out because so many men (especially the Betas) have dropped out of the dating game altogether, kind of like Ernie and his roommates at the beginning of Chapter 1 on the marriage strike.

With fewer available men to marry, many women

are left to live alone or have children by themselves. According to the *New York Times*, "more than half of births to American women under 30 occur outside marriage."[24] What price will these children and society pay when the kids grow up without a father or even a male role model because men are afraid to coach Little League for fear of being called a pervert? And if more women are bringing up kids without a father, they are likely to have fewer children. It's hard enough to raise one child alone, much less two or more. According to the *L.A. Times*:

> Births fell 4% from 2007 to 2009, the biggest drop for any two-year period since the mid-1970s, according to federal government data released Thursday.
>
> The rate, 66.7 births per 1,000 women ages 15 to 44, isn't the lowest in recent memory. The 1997 rate was an all-time low of 63.6. But the authors of the report say preliminary data show the birth rate continued falling through the first half of 2010.[25]

And it's not just in the United States that low birth rate is a problem; in fact, the U.S. birth rate is not that bad. Birth rates are falling even more in other countries. Jim Macnamara, in his book on *Media and Male Identity*,[26] mentioned a feature article published in the *Sydney Morning Herald* called, "So Who Wants to be a Father?" that examined Australia's falling birth rate. The female author, Leslie Cannold (who interviewed no men), described the anguish and anxiety of women who want to have children. She then declared that the falling birth rate was a "male problem." She concluded:

> The sort of bloke in short supply is the sort who doesn't throw up at the thought of love or even commitment, but looks quite capable of pulling off both should the need arise.[27]

So the author concludes incorrectly that the problem with low birth rate is *caused* by men who just don't want to commit; men's avoidance of fatherhood was addressed more correctly by a male reader who saw this article and wrote a letter to the editor of *Good Weekend Magazine*:

> Did Leslie Cannold ever think to ask men why they are fatherhood-phobic? Maybe a visit to the local pub where many fortysomething men have sorry tales to tell of wives who initiated divorces would be revealing. All they are left with are bitter memories and the sizeable financial burden of child support. No wonder the current crop of potential fathers is wary.[28]

Yes, part of the current birth decline is the recession, but even in 1997, the rates were low in the United States. Some of this is probably due, in some part, to men's reluctance to get involved with a system that gives them no incentive to marry and have children and actively punishes them if they do. How will these declining birth rates affect the future of the United States and other westernized countries? With fewer workers in the coming decades, who will provide services, work the jobs and pay into the already dwindling Social Security system?

With women raising kids alone by choice or otherwise, men will go off and do their own thing. Many will succeed and live a fine life, but others, mainly younger ones with fewer resources, may end up with few job skills or a dead-end job, little education, and feelings of alienation from society—which can lead to social instability. Men as a whole want to be doing things and taking risks that lead to innovation and economic growth, not hanging out all the time in the basement without purpose. As one of my insightful readers, David, said, "the issue of marginal men is something that should be looked at from the point of view of innovation and advancement being replaced by a stalled nation. A stalled nation has its men in idle. Highly active men in a town of 50,000 can do remarkable things—that's all the Renaissance was. What can a small town do when the street corner is littered with men and feral dogs? Risk aversion does not a 'Start-up Nation' make." No, it does not. Our nation will stagnate economically and culturally if we keep up this war on men.

Even if women pick up the slack, supporting the men on the margins will cost the country more than it can imagine, both economically and culturally. We need men's contributions: Without them, our nation will decline as a world leader, a beacon of hope of freedom, and as an economic force to be reckoned with. Perhaps those of a liberal persuasion will take some pleasure in this decline, but reality may bring forth a different sentiment. We need men's labor, their love of country and their sacrifice to survive; without it, we are at the mercy of those who wish to harm us; or maybe we will go down not with a bang, but with a whimper. Neither of these alternatives is a good one.

How can our society, because of a need for retribution, decide it is okay to waste men's potential? And are people really willing to sacrifice their little sons' emotional health and educational potential for the sake of revenge? Isn't that child abuse? One argument for feminism was that we were wasting the potential of half of humanity. We're no better off if we just waste the *other* half.

It's been nineteen years since Warren Farrell wrote his book, *The Myth of Male Power*, and more than ten years since Christina Hoff Sommers wrote *The War Against Boys*. These powerful books made a difference and started the conversation about the war against men and boys, but they are just the tip of the Italian iceberg. If anything, the culture has gotten worse in its degree of injustice and revenge tactics against men since these books were written. The acceptance of male-bashing and misandry in our society that I have outlined in the previous chapters suggests now is the time for action as opposed to discussion when it comes to men's rights, for no one is going to do anything about it without a fight. As Warren Farrell states, "Men must gather a new strength—the strength to fight the only world war in which the fodder is feelings. . . ."[29] How do you fight back? The next chapter will show you.

CHAPTER 6

Fighting Back, Going Galt or Both?

Revolution is a process, not an event.
—Anonymous

I was a victim who became a victor.
—Carnell Smith, a victim of paternity fraud who took his case all the way to the United States Supreme Court

So you've read the preceding pages and hopefully understand why men (and women) need to fight back. The time for silence and hand-wringing is over; the time for action has come. In this chapter, I will tell you how you can change your own life and, in turn, change society. I will be giving you tips and ideas of my own, but also I will be interviewing men and experts who have taken steps to reclaim justice for men and their pursuit of happiness as individuals in a free society. Some have taken small steps, others are large, but they are all important in winning the war against men that our society has been waging for so long. You can learn from these men and the following information or you can blaze your own path that will open the doors of liberty for all men.

Our sons, brothers, husbands, fathers and friends deserve no less.

Changing the culture and political landscape is hard; it takes patience, determination and an Army of Davids to gather steam to change the tide of injustice and prejudice against men that has been brewing now for more than forty years. People don't think of men as entitled to change; they believe that men have had it too good for too long, and that retribution is not only justified but also necessary. Though this is a myth, and society is willing to throw men under the bus for the "good of women" and the white knights who support them, we cannot let one type of inequity substitute for another.

Equality is not a zero-sum game where if one group has power, the others have less or none. We can strive for equality so that all people, including men, can live more productive and autonomous lives. Even in a politically correct article in the *Guardian* on how boys and men must be included in the conversation on equality (to help women, or course!), the author acknowledged, "there's something dangerously retributive about an approach that simply flips an inequity around and approaches power as a zero-sum game."[1] Men can't sit back any longer and let our female-privileged society continue down this road of revenge and retribution, for it will not end in a good place for men or society, as discussed in Chapter 5.

ACTION PLAN

So let's get started on an action plan with tips for fighting back in each of the areas that were discussed earlier in the book. These areas included marriage; paternity rights and forced fatherhood; education; advertising and a culture that portrays men in a negative light; and the decline of male space. The following tips may seem very general and they are, but the war against men is a very complex topic that requires some guidelines; these should be tweaked by individuals reading this book to fit with their own lives and abilities. It is beyond the scope of this book (which is meant to be a call to action rather than a research study) to address every area of discrimination against men, but I have highlighted what I think are the most important points from the book. Let's start with the most important tip.

TIP 1. Stop letting women run the agenda by controlling the dialogue on sex, gender, relationships and reproduction.

Men have just given the realm of sex, gender, relationships and reproduction over to women and left them to make the rules. No more. You must understand how powerful controlling the narrative is in these areas. If women make the decisions, *men* will be the ones living with these decisions. Men have no reproductive rights, and it's no wonder. If men concede that power exclusively to women, don't be surprised when men have no power.

Professor Jim Macnamara, in his study on men in the media, found that "the discourse on men and male identity reflected in and propagated through mass media editorials, opinion columns, features and letters, as well as comments quoted in news media articles, is largely contributed by women writers, academics and researchers. Furthermore, male voices given resonance in mass media discourse are, in most cases, pro-feminist men."[2]

When female-centered women and the Uncle Tims who go along with them are the *only* authority on men, fatherhood and sexuality, the agenda quickly pushes aside men's needs or rights, and allows injustice to flourish. I am not saying that all women present gender in unfair ways, but many are liberal academic types who are trying to set an agenda that keeps women's needs at the forefront and overlooks those of boys or men. Of course, there are women who are fair or sympathetic to men's needs, in addition to women's, but they are few and far between at this point in the media arena.

Takeaway lessons: Stop being silent. Silence leaves issues of sexuality and reproduction to be decided by women and the Uncle Tims and white knights who support them. If speaking up feels unnatural and is difficult, do it anyway. Remember that if people mock you, hate you and call you names when you speak out, that just means your message is working.

If you need help on speaking out, check out Richard Driscoll's book *You Still Don't Understand*,[3] which discusses communication techniques between men and women, or get a general book on how to communicate effectively, such as the old, but still relevant *Quick and Easy Way to Effective Speaking*[4] by Dale Carnegie. Other books that might help you are those that focus on how to get involved in government or politics and work at the grassroots level, and good ones to try are science-fiction writer Robert Heinlein's *Take Back Your Government*,[5] David Horowitz's *How to Beat the Democrats and Other Subversive Ideas*[6] or Saul Alinsky's *Rules for Radicals*.[7] Though Heinlein's book was originally written in 1946, it still has some good tips that are relevant, like "just show up." It's amazing how few people it takes on a local or state level to get things done. The latter two books are good from an overall tactical standpoint. Horowitz's book is obviously for Republicans and Alinsky's more for Democrats, but it's good to know both angles. In the war on men, though Democrats might be more likely to pass laws or engage in unjust laws and cultural norms against men, Republicans can often let their chivalry and white-knight impulses take over. So, plan on understanding what is involved in going after both sides.

If you feel you can't speak out, write. Go to blogs that discuss relationships, like TheFrisky.com relationship section,[8] or the men's section at YourTango.com[9] or other sites that focus on issues of men, women and relationships, and offer your comments. If these sites are filled with men's voices instead of just women's voices, other readers will find a different perspective instead of just the same old "men are bad, women are good" theme. Believe it or not, this small change can help change people's minds and open themselves up to other ideas if they see it enough. Remember what Mahatma Gandhi said: "First they ignore you, then they laugh at you, then they fight you, then you win."

TIP 2. Fight for better treatment of men in marriage and relationships.

This book is not a marriage or relationship manual, but there are a few things you need to know that I am going to tell you. First off, relationships are now all about emotional interactions and women are said to be better at controlling the emotional narrative. It doesn't have to be this way. Men are not the emotional wastelands that the media and culture would have you believe. Often they are just too afraid or pragmatic to say anything for fear of upsetting a woman. Also, many men are afraid they will not get laid if their wife or girlfriend is upset. Placating her, however, will probably have the opposite effect. So why put up with emotional abuse and go sexless?

You don't have to be rude, but *set boundaries* with your wife or girlfriend. The sooner, the better. If she is disrespectful, call her on it, even in front of friends. Women hate to be called out in public. Do this by saying that you will not have her act in a disrespectful manner toward you and that it is insulting. Talk to her later in private and tell her that you are happy to discuss problems or issues between the two of you, but insulting you or *demanding* that you follow her wishes is not acceptable.

You know the saying, "If mama ain't happy, ain't nobody happy." Well, it's not true. Your happiness matters too. Don't be an emotional hostage; start speaking up to your significant other about issues that concern you. Quit hiding in the basement with a beer and swallowing your anger or hurt over something she said.

As far as change in the laws of marriage and divorce to make it more equitable for men—this is a very tough one. Right now, women hold the cards in marriage, reproduction and divorce. Until change is implemented, men have a few choices: don't marry and stay single; live with a woman without marriage, but keep your eye on the common law or palimony laws, if any, in your state; or get married and learn how to get decent treatment in your relationship.

If you decide to get married, here are a few tips. Be sure. Date for a long time and live together if that goes along with your values. Two years or more is a good length of time to find out if you are compatible and to get a sense for her true personality. Find someone who earns approximately the same amount you do, or more if possible. That way, if you divorce, you will not be the one left holding the financial bag. If you work and your wife stays home with the kids, you must realize that you are more vulnerable if things don't work out. If you spend equal time with the kids, it makes it more likely that you will have a better case for more time with them if divorced. It's not great to have to think this way about what should be a trusting and loving relationship, but given the high divorce rate, protecting yourself throughout your dating life and marriage is just the reality for today's men. I have talked to men who were successful in getting divorced, meaning that they got custody of their children or kept at least half or more of their possessions. Those who won their cases did not let pride stand in their way. Pride is usually an excuse for doing nothing.

One divorced man I talked with said that his wife had cheated on him. He got the best recommendation for a lawyer that he could, had his wife followed by an investigator, got evidence that she was cheating and said to her face, "I will fight you for everything—the kids, the house, and the bank account." She backed down and he won his case and got custody of the kids. Many men think that they did something wrong or that if they had been more of a "man," the wife would not want a divorce. This type of pride will keep you from acting. Lose the pride.

In another successful case, Jerry, a forty-two-year-old African American male, who works as a personal trainer, told me that his ex-girlfriend tried to trap him into marriage by getting pregnant, though she said she was on the pill. They had broken up when she discovered she was pregnant, and, rather than wait until she went after him for child support, he took action. He went down to the child support agency after the child was born and showed them checks he had written for the child's care and asked to pay a reasonable amount of support himself. When the ex-girlfriend tried to go after him for more and then threatened him with domestic violence charges, he hired a lawyer and went after her. He found that she had an order of restraint taken out by a past boyfriend and used this to show that she herself was dangerous. He denied charges of domestic abuse and fought her every step of the way. The judge gave Jerry visitation and kept his child support the same. Jerry did not back down and won his case. Many men give up too easily. Don't be one of them.

Takeaway lessons: Set boundaries with your girlfriend or wife as early as possible. Once bad behavior starts, it is hard to change. If you find yourself in the middle of a divorce, lose the pride. Fight back, get a good lawyer and don't be afraid to take back what is yours. Quit the chivalry and inferiority complex that tells you that you weren't man enough and made the wife leave. It was her choice. I am always shocked by the men who tell me they lost everything in the divorce, but then find out that they never fought hard in the first place. If you try and still lose, at least you didn't sit back and do nothing.

I asked men's rights activist Glenn Sacks for some more tips for men on a state and national level, and here is what he said:

> It is important to understand that the system is not going to change by itself, or because it's unjust, or because it hurts children. It is only going to change if fatherhood and shared parenting advocates organize themselves into a strong, national organization that can compete in state capitols and DC with the National Organization for Women and its numerous allies. The Boston-based national group Fathers and Families has employed full-time legislative representatives and engaged in the political process on a professional level, and has had significant legislative success. They are organizing grassroots efforts in many states.[10]

Join and support some of these grassroots groups.

TIP 3. Fight for better laws, including those on paternity and forced fatherhood.

I contacted Carnell Smith, who runs a paternity fraud website at http://www.paternityfraud.com/ and his own website at CarnellSmith.com.[11] This man is a nonstop activist who has fought tirelessly for the past ten years on behalf of men who have been victims of paternity fraud. His story is a tragic one with a happy ending. From his website:

> Smith discovered that the child he loved and sup-
> ported for 11 years was in fact fathered by another
> man. Surprisingly the courts did not speak of restitu-
> tion nor of assigning responsibility to the biological
> father after hearing that the child's mother know-
> ingly and willfully withheld material facts from Smith.
>
> Instead Smith was told that it was his fault for not
> discovering the truth earlier and was bound by the
> courts to continue paying child support.[12]

Smith took his fight all the way up to the U.S. Supreme Court. His long fight took him from engineer to entre-preneur and activist for men's rights in paternity fraud:

> As Carnell Smith sought justice to save his family
> from poverty and homelessness, he also unearthed a
> desire to help others facing a similar situation.
>
> As the devastating numbers of children and
> parents affected by paternity fraud became more
> evident, Smith began to push for legislation that
> would protect Georgia's families. With the support
> of the Honorable Representative Stanley Watson,
> women, men, clergy, military victims, other law-
> makers, Smith successfully spear headed Georgia's
> first paternity fraud legislation in one year.

Determined to protect children and parents around the world, Smith also launched U.S. Citizens Against Paternity Fraud, a grassroots organization that educates and mobilizes voters around paternity, child support and custody laws.

Carnell Smith founded 4TRUTH Identity's DNA Center, providing genetic (DNA) tests similar to the one that transformed his life for maternity, paternity and immigration services.[13]

In an interview, I asked Mr. Smith how it was that he was successful in changing the laws in so many states to give men who were not the biological father the ability to disestablish paternity and stop paying child support for a child who was another man's. He responded that he approached the problem of paternity fraud to the courts and legislature as a "civil rights issue." That is, forcing a man to pay child support for another man's child whom he is not willing to adopt is defacto slavery. Smith also told me that he did not do it alone. "Women have got us beat socially. Men tend not to get out and make social connections the way women do." But Smith told me he had a great deal of help from others who cared about his cause. He was able to reach out and get them to help. In an email follow-up to our interview, Smith gave me more details on his case that readers might find helpful:

I used a two prong approach of continued litigation of my personal case while exposing "fact that family court does not operate as a court of law" while simultaneously lobbying for GA reform. Originally, I thought that winning my case at USCT [U.S. Supreme Court] would help other paternity fraud victims in other states. And believed that getting a new law in GA would help fellow Georgians overturn cases of paternity fraud. I was attempting to circumvent the need to lobby individual states to establish legal DNA testing to vacate cases of paternity fraud. Sadly, we are left with the only option to lobby individual states to reform paternity laws since USCT [U.S. Supreme Court] has refused to hear paternity fraud cases for more than ten years.

1. I took my case all the way to the USCT [U.S. Supreme Court], believing that "subject matter jurisdiction" is a proper defense to overturn a paternity judgment obtained by legal fraud or constructive fraud. The high court had two meetings about my case as representative of a national issue where states are allowed to disregard facts (mother's testimony/documents) and scientific evidence to forcibly maintain a fictional order of paternity.

   Results: USCT [U.S. Supreme Court] denied my appeal on June 9, 2002. Smith vs. Odum.

2. Due to continued lobby activity, national/
   local PR and majority public support, we were
   successful in getting GA House vote 163 to 0,
   GA Senate vote 45 to 5 and our Governor Roy
   Barnes signed HB369 (OCGA 19-7-54) into law
   on May 9, 2002.
3. Poetic Justice: I became the first victor to win his
   case using the new GA law 19-7-54 on Feb. 6,
   2003.

I believe that no person should have to face dis-
cretionary appeal where "prima facie evidence"
proves the accused male did not cause the pregnancy
as sworn by the child's mother.[14]

Takeaway lessons: Find one legislator or politician or
individual who is sympathetic to your cause, contact
him or her and meet with them to discuss what can
be done to change a specific law. Be willing to work
with others and don't discount people who are willing
to be involved. Smith said that 80 percent of the people who reach out to his organization are women: the
mothers, wives, sisters and even grandmothers of men
who have been deceived about the paternity of a child.
Be inclusive.

What about forced fatherhood through trickery;
what can you do about that? If you are long past caring,
what about your son? I went to the University of Tennessee to meet with Professor Higdon, who specializes

in family law, to get some tips. What I got also was a great hour-long discussion of the uphill battle that men are facing in terms of responsibilities for kids whom they didn't consent to having and a lesson about the lack of rights men have for a child who *is* his own.

Professor Higdon discussed the idea of coverture that now, he says, pertains to men instead of women. Coverture was part of the common law in England and the United States throughout the nineteenth century and was a "legal doctrine whereby, upon marriage, a woman's legal rights were subsumed by those of her husband."[15] "Whatever rights a man will hold is now held in *her* hands," Professor Higdon says. He gave examples of how men are financially liable for children who were conceived by trickery or even through child rape (a young boy assaulted by an older woman). He gave other examples of how a woman can give up a baby for adoption without consent; she does not have to name the father because of her right of privacy. The man can get on a putative father registry if he thinks that a woman is giving up his baby for adoption, but he must file in each state and it is easy for a woman to go to another state and give up *his* child. The registry is supposed to notify the man to tell him if the mother is coming to give up her child for adoption, but it is up to the man to track her down state-to-state. Professor Higdon shared a website, www.babyselling.com, about a father and his emotional roller coaster of trying to track down and keep his own child from being adopted.

According to Higdon, "we have reverted to this old system that feminists used to complain about where one gender held all the cards over the other . . . now we have reversed the genders. That's the irony to me. It also makes women look like lying harlots and teaches men to feel that way. It teaches men—always get a paternity test, even if you dated this woman since high school. It teaches men to stalk your ex-girlfriend so she can't move away and give the baby up for adoption because women are the type who will do this. That is the message it sends."

I asked Professor Higdon what advice he would give men to keep from getting tricked into a pregnancy. Here are some of his suggestions:

1. Don't have sex.
2. Get a vasectomy.
3. Use protection.
4. Keep said protection and destroy it when you are finished. Flush a condom and make sure it went down. There have been cases where women fished condoms out of the garbage or took the condom and used it to impregnate themselves.

For example, Joe Pressill is now the father of twins after his girlfriend stole his sperm by keeping a condom after they had sex and taking it to a fertility clinic to have them impregnate her. Then she sued him for child support.[16]

In another case, which was mentioned in Chapter 2, a man named Emile was visiting his sick parents in the hospital. A nurse, Debra, offered to have oral sex with him but only if he wore a condom. After the sexual encounter, Debra offered to dispose of the used condom. Nine months later, she gave birth to his child.[17]

I even read an article at AskMen.com entitled "Sperm-Jackers: The Five Types," which describes women for men to watch out for when finding sexual partners. Apparently, nonconsensual insemination is not all that rare.[18]

Takeaway lessons: Stop ignoring the fact that the new coverture is for men. Your life and decisions in many areas of reproductive and family life are now in the hands of women, whether you like it or not. The current laws and family courts dictate it. I hear men discuss how "manly" they are as they "do not care" about such things, it's "women's stuff." As author Michael Walzer, paraphrasing a quote by Leon Trotsky, once said, "you may not be interested in war, but war is interested in you."[19] A man doesn't put his head in the sand. *Denial can mean enslavement* down the road.

Learn the laws in your state about what your reproductive rights are and educate yourself. Yes, it is difficult and complicated, but it is worth doing as no one else will do it for you. Hopefully, as men demand more for themselves, educators on reproductive rights will come forward to educate the average man. Once men are educated, it seems hard to believe that they will allow themselves to be basically wage slaves and second-class citizens.

Demand a paternity test and make sure you are the dad if you are not married. And if you are married and not sure, do it also. Perhaps men should press for laws that mandate a paternity test at birth for all children, though some people (men included) see this as an invasion of privacy. However, given how few rights men have and how important paternity rights are, maybe it is not a bad idea.

TIP 4. Fight back in education.

Robert L. Shibley is the vice president of the Foundation for Individual Rights in Education (FIRE), an organization that is dedicated to fighting for freedom in colleges and universities. From their website, more specifically, FIRE's mission is:

> To defend and sustain individual rights at America's colleges and universities. These rights include freedom of speech, legal equality, due process, religious liberty, and sanctity of conscience—the essential qualities of individual liberty and dignity. FIRE's core mission is to protect the unprotected and to educate the public and communities of concerned Americans about the threats to these rights on our campuses and about the means to preserve them.[20]

I contacted Shibley to get some advice for men who are dealing with misandry, discrimination and a lack of due process in colleges today. I had corresponded with Shibley before for my blog, so I contacted him by email[21] and asked if he would answer some questions about how men are doing in college. Here are my questions and his answers:

HELEN SMITH: What do you think of the Office of Civil Rights curtailing the due process rights of the accused in sexual assault cases on campuses of those colleges accepting federal funds?

ROBERT SHIBLEY: FIRE has been opposing the curtailment of due process rights in the April 4, 2011, "Dear Colleague" letter from OCR from the very beginning. The letter requires that all universities subject to Title IX institute a low "preponderance of the evidence" standard for cases of sexual harassment or assault, and also requires that those accused be subjected to double jeopardy. Both fly in the face of centuries of American legal tradition and of justice itself. The proper way to address sexual assault on campus is not to make it easier to convict *anyone* accused of sexual assault, but to improve procedures so that when someone commits a sexual assault, students can be confident that the person being caught and punished for it actually committed the crime.

HS: What can men do to fight back against this?

RS: Men and women should engage with campus administrators to make it clear that students want to be treated as if they are innocent until proven guilty and that they do not want to be tried twice or more for the same offense. In addition, people who have been unjustly convicted of sexual assault by campus courts should get a lawyer and/or contact FIRE.

HS: What is the worst case you have had at FIRE that involved a man who was denied his rights? How was it handled?

RS: The worst case was that of Caleb Warner, a student at the University of North Dakota, who was convicted by a campus tribunal of sexual assault using the preponderance of the evidence standard, suspended for three years, and prohibited from taking classes at any North Dakota public college. Only a couple of months after he was thrown off campus, however, the Grand Forks, N.D., police department charged his accuser for making a false report about the alleged assault to law enforcement. (She is still wanted on this charge and has reportedly fled the state.) When Warner's lawyer brought this up to UND, UND refused to rehear his case. When they contacted FIRE and FIRE wrote to UND about it,

UND stated that there was no new evidence and that they simply determined that Warner was guilty of sexual assault using the very same evidence that the police used to charge Warner's *accuser* with lying to them. Only after FIRE exposed this outrage in the *Wall Street Journal* did UND relent, reconsider the case, and "vacate" the punishment. But UND has never apologized or even acknowledged that they got the case totally wrong.

HS: How can men in general fight back in an atmosphere in colleges where they are discriminated against with the authority of the college administration? For example, forced sexual harassment training, etc.?

RS: The best way is by exercising their right to protest and organize on campus against these measures. Universities rely on their students meekly complying with their rules, no matter how Orwellian or intrusive. If students are aware of their rights and demand that they be respected, it is much harder for a university to intrude upon them. This is particularly true because universities cannot defend in public or in the media what they do to their students in private.

HS: Do you have any ideas or advice for men on how to speak up in colleges or universities without fear of getting their grades cut or expelled?

One excellent way is by contacting FIRE and letting us know about what you plan to do, so that if it results in punishment FIRE can go into action more quickly. Generally, though, organization and numbers are important. It's easy to punish one student, especially if that student doesn't know about FIRE; it's much harder to silence a student organization—even a small one. And going to the press in cases of censorship always makes a university much more careful about what it's doing. Universities rely on good PR for their donations, and they therefore take bad PR quite seriously.

HS: Do you have any thoughts for how parents can protect their sons from colleges that discriminate against men?

RS: Parents should demand answers from colleges who have policies that discriminate against men (or anyone else). College administrators take the opinion of parents seriously, and a call or letter to them will certainly be read. And if they don't like the answers they're getting, they should seriously consider talking with their children about switching to a new school and letting the school know why they're doing it. Money, as always, talks the loudest.

HS: Do you think it helps for men to speak out freely in schools where they may face repercussions? Or is it better to lie low until one is out of school? Is there a middle ground, such as writing stealth papers, research, etc., that tackle a topic such as men's issues in a more indirect way? E.g., do a research paper on the effects of paternity fraud on men's feelings and emotions, rather than tackle writing on why women who commit paternity fraud should be punished, etc.?

RS: What helps the most is for men to be educated on the issues about which they've chosen to speak. Simply expressing crude or "un-PC" opinions makes it easy for a university to characterize a man as sexist or outside the mainstream. But it's very difficult for administrators to come down hard on those with good, well-formed, reasoned points. While colleges would often like to pretend that all "right-thinking" people must agree with their viewpoints, they are aware that off-campus, there are literally millions of Americans who disagree with them on virtually any given issue. And many of those dissenters pay taxes or tuition to support their campus jobs! It's one thing to pick a fight with a largely powerless student—it's another to be willing to tell the public at large that half of them are sexists, racists, or bigots of some description.

Takeaway lessons: Don't sit back and let the university dish out whatever politically correct regulations it decides on. Start a small, vocal group and get the media involved if possible. Notice that it was only when FIRE exposed the Warren case in the *Wall Street Journal* that the University of North Dakota relented. If you need guidance, contact FIRE at 215-717-FIRE (3473) or visit their website at http://thefire.org/about/contact/.

TIP 5. Fight back against negative portrayals of men in the media and culture.

First off, control your own behavior. Stop laughing when men are beaten and bruised by women for things like cheating or just because some women are violent. It's understandable that comedy skits like slapstick are funny, but when you laugh at another man who is going through hell, you make the situation worse and perpetuate the stereotype that it's okay to abuse men, especially when women do it. I once wrote about a story of a college guy who was beaten with a baseball bat by his girlfriend, also a student, for breaking up with her. Everyone thought it was hilarious, even other men. That's disturbing, and if you think it's worth laughing at, you have no one to blame but yourself when men are treated badly.

If you see other men laughing at such things, say something. You don't have to be a wimp about it. Mock them mercilessly. I often call them Uncle Tims for selling out their own gender. Men don't like being made fun of, but sometimes it's the only way to get them to stop male-bashing and belittling other men.

Takeaway lessons: If you see shows or ads that bash

men, go to the website or find out the phone number of the sponsor of that ad and email them about your concern. Tell them you will not buy their products because they are misandrists who bash men. Don't buy their products or services. Money talks. You would be surprised how effective a dozen complaints from men would be. Men's rights advocate Glenn Sacks has organized campaigns against a number of shows and ads that bash men and has been quite effective.

TIP 6. Reclaim male space.

Men's groups have been marginalized to the point where men are often afraid to have any group that is specified as a group for men. Think of universities where they often have a women's center but almost never a men's center. I was surprised to learn of a men's law group at one of the large public universities and tracked down the president, Matt. We met at the law school one day and I asked him how the men's law group came about.

"A couple of years ago, we noticed that there were all these groups at our school—the Black Law students, the Women Law Students, the Latino Law Students—so we decided that the administration could not turn us down when we went to set one up. They didn't seem to like it but they let us have it. It's like they judge it in some way." Even though the group is not about men's rights, but mainly for men to do charity work and get together for some male bonding activities such as dinner, shooting and golf, there were some people at the law school who did not like the fact that the men had a group. "Our group rubs people the wrong way," Matt stated. "Some of the liberal women find it demeaning." When I asked why, Matt said he didn't really know other than they might be seen as sexist. "We have to be really careful about what we say or we could get disciplined. I have heard of other male undergrad groups having that happen to them."

"Wow," I thought, "these universities are real treasure troves of free speech"—but on with the story and the stealth way that these law men have asked for their male space and put it to use. Yes, women can join, just as men can join the women's group or any other group. There are about eighty-six members, with two women who occasionally come to some of the dinners or go out for drinks. The law group does some charity work for other men, such as collecting cell phones for veterans or helping to raise money for a local young men's group that has an after school program that provides recreation to keep boys from joining gangs. The group even ran in a 5K to support heart disease research because one of the male students had died from a heart condition. Their outside activities also include doing guy things, such as going to restaurants for large portions of steak and going out to smoke cigars. In this group setting outside of the university, they could joke and have fun without worrying too much about saying the wrong thing. "You don't want to say the wrong thing or stick out at school. If you don't say anything, it's hard to interpret."

There are very few men's law groups in the nation, but there should be more. I was dismayed, though not at all surprised, that a men's group had to watch what they said in the law school, but the amazing fact here is that a group of men wanted to have a presence in the school and they got the administration to act on their wishes. Just the presence of the group is a statement: "We are men and we are here. This is a space carved out in this school for us." One reason that Matt felt there weren't more men's law groups is that men don't ask. If you make a case to the administration, they typically have to let men have the group if others already do. Though they may not like it, they typically must let students set one up.

Takeaway lessons: If you want more male space, ask for it. Even if it is not ideal, a male presence will make a difference and start on the road to men being fully back out in the public sphere. As far as home goes, don't slink down to a man cave unless this is a space that you truly want and desire. If your wife demands that you take the dirty garage or some dingy basement while the rest of the family enjoys the run of the house, make it a point to talk with her about your need for space. If she balks at you, let her know that this is important to you and if you need space and it is not available at home, you may have to be in the office more or out in your car to get some decent space.

WHAT ABOUT GOING GALT?

Remember that in the introduction I talked about going Galt, which is a metaphor for withdrawing your talents from the world and turning inward to keep from being exploited. In today's modern world, going Galt may be a bit different than what Ayn Rand had in mind in *Atlas Shrugged*, but the idea is similar. Why should you put out your best effort only to have it taken from you by the government, the state, women or by the matriarchy-by-proxy set? By the latter term, I mean those politicians and legislators who may be male but who carry out what women's groups or their supporters want in terms of the law or special privileges that are generally unfair to men and put women in a protected or privileged position.

Many men have started to go Galt by refusing to marry, thereby not being involved in that particular group of laws and system by opting out. If you are living with a woman, do make sure that you watch out for laws in some states that have common law marriages or palimony laws so that you don't end up being caught by surprise with legal responsibilities that you did not intend. This is one possibility.

Another way to go Galt is to live on your own terms, make enough money to get by, and stay out of the system's way. I have noticed a number of men in my hometown who get joy out of driving around, drinking beer, and working on their own hobbies in peace and tranquility in their own homes or in homes they share with other guys. They don't have to worry about going down to the man cave as they have the run of the house, or that their hobby will be shelved or stopped because of a spouse's refusal to allow it. For some men, this works. For others, it may not. But even married men can go Galt within reason. Of course, if you have a family, you will have to consider everyone's needs in your decision to go Galt.

I asked men on my blog for some examples of how they might go Galt in a female-centered society. Here are some responses.

Stephenlclark wrote in:
There are still many jobs for men. You want something hands-on then look at the energy boom in places like the Dakotas and elsewhere for example, the world still runs on machines that need servicing; most working at these jobs are men and likely to remain so. There will always be a need for welders! These jobs pay well, and if you know a second language and are willing to travel there's that too. One of [the] busiest guys I've met here in rural Missouri worked on helicopter engines [and] traveled to jobs all the time. At least in the rural areas, there are opportunities for small businesses that service homeowners and always will be.

If the university is your thing then focus on engineering degrees—for all the desire to increase female engineering enrollments it's still no higher than about 30% except in rare instances. Employment of engineering grads is still good and will continue to be so and the comment about language ability and travel applies here particularly.

Lastly, open your eyes and look beyond the boundaries of the US: it's a great big world out there, a frontier where PC-mavens neither rule nor exist. Learn a skill, learn another language and go: You are endowed by your Creator with the unalienable right to pursue happiness. Pursue it.[22]

JKB says:

Not every way of "going Galt" is workable for every man. I would say, though, that men should adopt the habits used traditionally by Jews as they lived and worked in societies that were or had potential of becoming hostile to them. These are, in fact, survival skills of any group not secure in their surroundings.

Concentrate on mobile wealth, pursue independent businesses rather than jobs that leave you at the whim of some individual or small group of individuals, develop journeyman skills (journeyman in the original sense of working by the day or contract), and focus on marketable skills that depend on your knowledge, which can't be seized, over credentials which can be rendered worthless.[23]

Eric R. wrote in:

One other thing men could do to go Galt: Don't enlist in the military. Why put your life on the line for a system that treats you as a second class citizen?[24]

Armageddon Rex says:

I agree with Eric R. but his idea is incomplete. Carry it a step further. In every traditional society men are the protectors against external and internal enemies. Since men no longer enjoy full and equal citizenship in our society, it's time society reaped the crop they've planted. I will encourage, and I urge all other men in western societies who work with and train boys and young men to likewise encourage the males they encounter to NOT join the military, NOT to become any kind of peace officer or work in Law Enforcement or Corrections in any way, and NOT to become a firefighter, EMT or Paramedic. I would encourage them to boycott studying obstetrics as well, but our current usurious, litigation happy society is already taking care of that. . . . [25]

These are just some suggestions. Think of some of your own and see what comes to mind. One point I want to make on the latter two suggestions by Eric R. and Armageddon Rex is that some men are already thinking about no longer allowing themselves to be placed in positions that are dangerous in order to protect others. Why should they fight and possibly die for a culture that sees them *both* as expendable and like second-class citizens? Like the *Concordia* shipwreck captain and crew that was discussed in Chapter 4, men are heading for the exits and asking "Dude, where's *my* lifeboat?" When society viewed men as important and heroic for taking on these roles and treated them with more fairness and respect, men were willing to step up. Many still are, but I wonder for how long?

USE A COMBINATION OF APPROACHES THAT WORK FOR YOUR PERSONALITY TYPE

You can use a combination of one or more of these approaches—either fighting back, going Galt or both, or individualize them and find out what works best for you based on what type of person you are. Are you a behind-the-scenes kind of guy? Perhaps yelling for your rights won't work for you, but you could write for, or work for, a political campaign that you believe in, or write opinion pieces for the web or other media. Find some that are inclusive of men's points of view but don't be shy about trying to get to those that frown on such things. A bit of controversy might up their readership and they might be willing to take a piece on gender and sexuality from a guy.

If you are a person who likes being in the spotlight, use the media to your advantage. This is what Carnell Smith, the paternity rights activist, did, and it worked beautifully for him. He told me he once got men from all over the country to come to the state capital in Georgia with signs that read, "Why does our government want men to be homeless?" in response to unfair paternity fraud cases where men are going broke trying to pay for kids who are not even their own. He then sent out press releases and called the media to come down and film the protest.

If you have a local community-access television station in your town, go to the city hall or school board meetings and ask to speak. They will usually give you a few minutes of air time and you can share your grievance on a local men's issue that may concern you. For example, if the schools have incorporated some kind of propaganda against males in the curriculum like the *Miss Representation* film presented in Chapter 4 and your son or daughter is being affected, go and tell them about it. Ask the school board members why your local school (call the school out by name) discriminates against boys and give some examples. If you also shame the board members by calling them out by name, so much the better. Anyway, you hopefully get the idea and can come up with some ways, no matter how small, to improve the lives of yourself and other men and boys in your community.

DEALING WITH ANGRY WOMEN, WHITE KNIGHTS AND UNCLE TIMS

Since these groups are so prevalent, they require a section all to themselves. These three groups are the biggest deterrents to men standing up for themselves, so how do you deal with people from these groups? If you can understand them and find out their motivations, it will help you figure out the best course of action.

Women who are angry and complain a lot seem to get help—both in the media and in their relationships with others. Women tend to be more willing to "initiate relationship conflict, more willing to escalate conflict, better able to handle it when it occurs and quicker to recover from it."[26] Men tend to be more stressed and confused in angry confrontations with their significant others and tend to withdraw and stonewall.[27]

The problem with this approach is that it leads to marital dissatisfaction and possible divorce because the man's stress is a leading indicator of dissatisfaction with a marriage.[28] If you are dealing with an angry woman whom you care about, try talking to her about what you feel. Let her know that you feel upset by her words and need some time to cool off. Once you feel better about things, talk with her, stay involved and try to talk it out. Women often get angry because their anger is their power with a man. He will try to do what he can to placate or help her. This was perhaps necessary in times past as women had little in the way of power and they needed their husbands to listen. Now that women hold the power, maybe they need to try to listen a little bit more.

What about all of the angry women in the world, like the vicious types who think of men as enemies that are belittling and abusive? Call them on it. Women hate being called out in front of others; if a woman is rude to you or belittling in public, call her an emotional abuser in front of others or in a blog comment. Nothing will bother her more than being told she is acting in an abusive manner: Most women like to think of themselves as an emotionally competent person who could be a victim, but not a victimizer. Use your own form of operant conditioning, meaning that there are some consequences to making belittling, sexist statements with little thought. This could be a cold stare, withdrawing from the conversation, or thinking of a clever comeback such as "gee, you're a real treat"—something that lets her know her statements are out of line. At work, it's a different matter and it's probably best to avoid these types if possible or work in an all-male industry if you feel you cannot be around women like this.

White knights and Uncle Tims are both types of men who elevate women to a privileged position in different ways, often for different reasons. The white knight wants to take care of women and sees her as a damsel in distress who needs his masculine protection to get by. His status rises because he is seen by some men as chivalrous and by women as a protector. If he is a politician, he might be more conservative and will see certain unfair laws against men as necessary to protect the little women from the big bad wolf—men, of course. Realize that this guy wants to be seen as a hero, but you must treat him as a fool. This will humiliate him and get him to rethink his chivalrous tendencies, which often lead to men being harmed and women gaining privilege. If you encounter a white-knight type in Internet chat rooms or out in the world, call him out for being a tool of women, for that's what he is.

An Uncle Tim is generally a sellout to his own gender who is more than likely either a politician type—usually liberal—or just a guy trying to get laid who thinks that his PC behavior will get him laid more often. Point this out as frequently as possible and make fun of him for it. Shaming him is vital. The Uncle Tim type might just be a young guy who has been brainwashed into believing that he must dance to the "female as superior" tune as men must be punished for discrimination against women in the past. In this case, try to educate him or give him some reading materials on the Internet or elsewhere to show him where he is going wrong, or pray he grows out of it. If he continues past the age of thirty, shame him also. Once the mocking reaches a level where it is uncomfortable to speak up about how men must pander to women, he will probably stop or at least think twice about it.

TIPS FOR WOMEN ON HOW TO HELP

While working with men and working on this book, I have met many women who really care about men and

about justice. Though the media would have you believe
that any man who dares speak about his rights is a mi-
sogynist and all women are victims with few rights and
a list of grievances that have never been resolved, not all
women feel this way. Many are open-minded and love
their fellow man and want things to be fair. For example, my friend and fellow blogger, Amy Alkon, speaks
up for men on her blog, www.advicegoddess.com. She
gives advice to women and men, and her blog is straight-
forward and helpful to both. If women try to act like
victims, she calls them on it. If men are having issues in
a relationship, she doesn't assume *he's* the bad guy. We
need more women like Alkon in the relationship arena
who stand up for *both* genders.

So what can women do to increase positive interactions with men? Here are my top three suggestions:

1. Stop your natural tendency to complain to him
   so much. Yes, the culture tells you to do it and
   the media exacerbates female victimhood and
   misandric behavior, *but stop it*. If your husband
   or boyfriend has flaws, you don't have to always
   point them out. Try to focus on his more positive
   qualities. If he fixes things around the house or
   acts as a bodyguard at night, remember that those
   duties are just as, or sometimes more, important
   than washing the dishes.

2. Do not go out and *complain about him to others*.

This is a killer for your relationship, and if he finds out you are hanging out with your girl-friends and dissing him, his feelings of trust will break down. And if your girlfriends constantly complain about men, tell them that you don't appreciate it. If you fear they will ostracize you for that, they aren't very good friends. And if you care more about your friends' feelings than your husband's or boyfriend's feelings, then how important can your relationship be?

3. Listen without judgment to what your guy has to say. People are always saying that men don't speak up, but they often don't because of the negative reaction they get, especially from women. Men are terrified of angry, judgmental women. So, no matter how weird or disturbing you think of what your husband or boyfriend says, listen and don't interrupt with how he *should* feel. Just let him talk. At the same time, don't try to get him to talk about your relationship constantly; this is a relationship killer.

WHERE DO WE GO FROM HERE?

This short book has taken a look at why men are on strike in our society and tried to provide some solutions. However, while fighting back on an individual level is good, there is much more that needs to be done on a system-wide level. Many of the young men I talked with, and even the older ones, seemed to have no clue about their lack of rights in the areas we discussed. They were shocked to learn that they had no or very few reproductive rights, that the family court didn't care if their wife cheated in a divorce or that they could be held to a fairly low standard at college should they be charged with a sexual assault.

And as for what complex legal terms like coverture mean? Forget it. Most men, even educated ones, have no idea. But they should, because they are living the modern twenty-first century version of it, just with the genders switched. Now women (and the state) hold the legal and psychological cards, and men are just now figuring it out. A man may pretend that it doesn't matter or that he is too "masculine" to care, but his denial doesn't make the truth—that he has little control over his legal fate in reproduction, sexual harassment law or marriage—any less real.

The first thing that needs to be done is to educate boys and men about their legal rights (or lack thereof). This could be done through boys' and men's organizations or private means. Parents should agitate school systems by high school for health classes that provide speakers who can talk explicitly on what men and boys face in the legal arena and how to protect themselves. We need more classes on men and the law to educate future lawyers and others about men's issues who, in turn, would provide guidance to other men on how to navigate the system and fight back. Education is a start, but it is only a beginning.

There has been talk of a White House Council on Boys and Men, but one has to wonder if government involvement might cause more problems. If this council is done correctly, it might be effective in providing a large-scale study of how boys are doing in education, college and the community and provide some guidance to schools about how to more effectively engage boys and young men. The proposal for the council was put together by Warren Farrell, who is indeed a friend to men and boys, so it just might be okay. There is a website that describes the council at http://whitehouseboysmen.org/blog/. You might want to look at it and see what you think.

We need more systematic studies that look at how men actually cope with many of the issues that we have touched on. For example, how are men dealing with paternity fraud? Carnell Smith, the activist described earlier in this chapter, is working with a sociologist on such a study of men's emotions and feelings when finding out they are not the father of a child. These studies need to become part of the conversation and input when deciding paternity or family law, just as women's attitudes and feelings about rape have a huge impact on public policy.

Why is there no *extremely active* National Organization of Men or American Association of University Men? There should be. Warren Farrell is the co-president of The National Organization for Men[29] but I had never heard of it until I looked it up on the Internet. It should be a household word. Maybe in days past there was no reason for such an organization but there is now, more than ever, for men are in the minority in colleges and many aspects of American life. Yes, I know; there are some men in high positions. Seriously, though, there are very few in comparison to the entire male population. As Scott Adams, the author of the *Dilbert* cartoons, says of men in top positions, "THOSE ARE OTHER MEN."[30]

The average man has no lobby and few advocates. This needs to change. With individuals fighting back and lobbies to advocate for men, only then will we begin to see change. As men's rights activist Glenn Sacks told me in an interview, "Men must have effective, well-funded, professional organizations that lobby for them at the state capitol and in Washington, D.C., just like the feminists."[31] I wish it could be different and that men could just get a fair shake because the country was fair. But it's not, and wishing it so will not work. So far, everyone is just telling men to "grow a pair" or "man up," which are just buzz words for "do what we want and don't give us any trouble." Don't listen. Speak up. Fight back. Support a good men's-advocacy group. Men in a free society deserve no less.

This book is meant mainly to be a wake-up call about the need for change and advocacy in the area of men's rights and men's issues. If you would like to discuss or read more on this topic, visit my blog at www.pjmedia .com/drhelen or email me at askdrhelen@hotmail.com.

Conclusion

Many years ago, I lived in New York City for graduate school and I worked as a psychologist for the state. My favorite pastime while walking to work or school was to stop and watch the construction workers building these incredible high structures all across the city. Sometimes they were just working on old buildings to make sure they were in good repair. I would stand with wonder and watch the men as they balanced on beams, hosed down sidewalks, and handled heavy material like it was nothing. Though you might want to get Freudian here and think that I had some kind of penis envy—the hose and all—my feeling was one of admiration, not envy. I was grateful that these men were willing to build such incredible structures at the risk of their own life so that I, and my fellow New Yorkers, might have a better one.

By the time I got to work or school, however, the sentiment of my fellow New Yorkers about the construction workers was not so positive. Often, women would complain that the men yelled out some kind of compliment or leer such as "looking good" or they would smack their lips. I can understand that this is not welcome for most women, who just want to get to work or school without a leering squad. However, this is the only quality that these women remembered about the construction workers or men around the city who were providing services to them on a daily basis; the men's better qualities and what they were doing escaped them. Many of the women were very angry and wanted something done about the men looking at them on the street. Gathering them up and putting them in jail for simply looking was fair justice for some of these women.

I look around every day at the wonder of men, how many of them are the building blocks of our society, quietly going about their day around my office planting trees and doing the landscaping, or mowing lawns, running businesses that hire people, working as doctors to help people get better, or just making society a better place by their perseverance and abilities. But mainly what our society focuses on now is the negative traits that they perceive men to have. Misandry is so common that no one even questions it. Writer Camille Paglia offers a refreshing exception to this disparagement of men, as pointed out by Christina Hoff Sommers:

> For Paglia, male aggressiveness and competitiveness are animating principles of creativity: "Masculinity is aggressive, unstable, and combustible. It is also the most creative cultural force in history." Speaking of the "fashionable disdain for 'patriarchal society' to

which nothing good is ever attributed," she writes, "But it is the patriarchal society that has freed me as a woman. It is capitalism that has given me the leisure to sit at this desk writing this book. Let us stop being small-minded about men and freely acknowledge what treasures their obsessiveness has poured into culture." "Men," writes Paglia, "created the world we live in and the luxuries we enjoy": "When I cross the George Washington Bridge or any of America's great bridges, I think—*men* have done this. Construction is a sublime male poetry."[1]

Our society has become the angry leered-at woman who doesn't care that men can build buildings or do amazing things like be good dads, husbands and sons. She focuses instead on the small flaws that some men have and extrapolates to all men; they are all dogs, rapists, perverts, deadbeats and worthless. Who needs them?

We do. Our society has forgotten the wonder of men in its quest for retribution against men and boys who often weren't even alive when women were being discriminated against. Many men understand the war that is going on against them and they are going underground or withdrawing their talents and going on strike in marriage, fatherhood, education and in society in general. They may not speak about it or use a megaphone to let the world know of their pain, frustration and anger, or just plain apathy, but it is there—raw and just underneath the surface. We as a society must wake up to what we are doing to men before it is too late and we live in a world that has left male potential in a wasteland.

Our society is made better by men who are productive, happy and treated with fairness. We have only ourselves to blame if we do not turn the tide of the war on men, for without half the human experience, our society can crumble, just as surely as those New York buildings would if they no longer had men to work their sublime male poetry on them. Is that the world you want to live in? I don't.

Acknowledgments

I am indebted to the thousands of readers I have had over the years at www.drhelen.blogspot.com and www.pjmedia.com who have read and commented on probably thousands of posts and sent hundreds of emails giving me insight into how the male mind ticks. Many of you know who you are and some, but not all, have asked that your names not be used, but I do want to thank you because without my readers and those men who so graciously shared their lives and feelings with me, I would not have been able to put this book together. I am also grateful for all of the clients I have had over my many years of practice who helped me to understand more deeply what it is to be male in modern American culture.

Thanks very much to Encounter Books for giving me the opportunity to write about the men's issues that I hold so dear. I am especially grateful to Roger Kimball, who never doubted that men would be interested in this topic when other publishers told me that only women cared about issues of gender rights, relationships, marriage and culture. "Men," they said, "don't buy such books." I hope this book proves them wrong and, more important, sets the stage for other authors and activists who can take this fight to the next level. Special thanks also to Katherine Wong, Lauren Miklos and Elaine Ruxton at Encounter Books.

Thanks very much to my friends and colleagues who have helped and encouraged me to write this book. Amy Alkon had been ever cheerful and encouraging and readily shared her ideas on men's issues over the years. Vox Day was quick to help with his keen insights on why men don't marry, and shared his illustrations and data that added to this discussion of how men see the world. Thanks to Stacy Campfield, Michael J. Higdon, Glenn Sacks and Carnell Smith for changing the landscape of the men's rights field, for fighting for justice, and for providing me with material for this book. Special thanks to Sophia Brown for preparing my manuscript.

I am especially indebted to Christina Hoff Sommers, who shared her immense knowledge on men and college with me and who knew what was coming down the pike more than ten years ago. Stephen Baskerville also added his insight into the marriage and divorce industry, which was most helpful. I am also grateful to Robert Shibley and his organization, FIRE, which fights back against discrimination and stands up for free speech in college and university settings.

Finally, I am grateful to my family, who listened to me talk for years about men's rights—sometimes to the point where I was really annoying—but they listened anyway. Thanks to Janet, Walter, Kathy, Joey and Anne for their time.

But most of all, thanks to my husband, Glenn Reynolds, and daughter, Julia, who not only listened to all my talk about men's rights but also called me on it when I wasn't following through on my ideology. Only they know what I am talking about here, and I will leave it at that.

Resources for Men

I have included some books and websites here that will help men and their supporters increase their knowledge about how to cope with being male in the twenty-first century.

RECOMMENDED BOOKS

Christina Hoff Sommers, *The War Against Boys: How Misguided Feminism Is Harming Our Young Men*, New York: Simon & Schuster, 2001.
This book gives a good overview of the problems that boys are having in education. If you have a son in the school system, this is a good book to give you an idea of what your child might be dealing with as a boy or young man.

Warren Farrell, *The Myth of Male Power*, New York: Simon & Schuster, 1993.
This book will help you understand in more detail why men don't actually have the kind of power that feminists claim.

Warren Farrell, *Women Can't Hear What Men Don't Say: Destroying Myths, Creating Love*, New York: Tarcher, 2000.

This is a good relationship book to get some tips on how to communicate more effectively with your wife or significant other.

Richard Driscoll, *You Still Don't Understand*, Knoxville, Tenn.: Westside Psychology, 2009.

This is a great book on the differences between men and women in relationships and can help the reader understand how to cope with angry or manipulative women.

Stephen Baskerville, *Taken into Custody: The War Against Fathers, Marriage, and the Family*, Nashville, Tenn.: Cumberland House Publishing, 2007.

Baskerville is a political scientist who describes the totalitarian divorce industry in the United States that abuses parents and children, runs rampant over civil liberties and is accountable to no one.

Paul Nathanson and Katherine K. Young, *Legalizing Misandry: From Public Shame to Systemic Discrimination Against Men*, Montreal: McGill-Queen's University Press, 2006.

This book gives a detailed overview of the discrimination men face in our society.

Mystery's *The Pickup Artist: The New and Improved Art of Seduction*, New York: Villard, 2010, or Neil Strauss' *The Game: Penetrating the Secret Society of Pickup Artists*, New York: It Books, 2005.
Both of these books are good if you need some tips and understanding of how to date and pick up women. They are especially good for men who are shy or need a boost of confidence when approaching women.

Jim Macnamara, *Media and Male Identity: The Making and Remaking of Men*, New York: Palgrave Macmillan, 2006.
This is a terrific study looking at the negative portrayal of men in the media.

WEBSITES
www.carnellsmith.com and www.paternityfraud.com/
Sites on paternity fraud. If you are the victim of paternity fraud or know someone who is, these sites are great resources.

www.glennsacks.com
This website is run by men's rights activist Glenn Sacks and focuses on men, fatherhood, divorce and custody issues.

http://www.marriedmansexlife.com/
This is Athol Kay's website on how married men can
improve their sex lives using game.

www.ArtofManliness.com.
Brett McKay and his wife, Kate, have some good tips
and ideas for men on how to cope with being a male in
today's society.

http://thefire.org/
The Foundation for Individual Rights in Education.
This is an organization that defends and sustains
individual rights at America's colleges and universities.

http://www.fathersandfamilies.org/
"Fathers and Families promotes an ambitious legislative
agenda and has helped pass family court reform
legislation in over two dozen states."

About the Author

Helen Smith is a psychologist specializing in forensic issues and men's issues in Knoxville, Tennessee. She holds a PhD from the University of Tennessee and master's degrees from The New School for Social Research and the City University of New York. She has written *The Scarred Heart: Understanding and Identifying Kids Who Kill* and is the writer and executive producer of *Six*, a documentary about the murder of a family in Tennessee by teens from Kentucky. She has worked with men (as well as women and children) in her private practice for more than twenty years.

She has been on numerous television and radio shows, including *Montel Williams*, and has appeared on E! Entertainment, Fox News, Discovery, Women's Entertainment, Biography, Oxygen and the Learning Channel. Smith has written for numerous publications, including the *L.A. Times*, the *Christian Science Monitor* and *The Cleveland Plain Dealer*. She occasionally hosts a show at PJTV.com focusing on men's issues, psychology and politics. She has written on her blog at www.drhelen

.blogspot.com since 2005 on men's rights, men's issues and psychology and is now a columnist and blogger at PJ Media at www.pjmedia.com.

Her blog is at www.pjmedia.com/drhelen.

Notes

Preface to the Paperback Edition

1. Letter to the author from Christian, January 1, 2014.
2. Randy Wallace, "Father Pays Outstanding Child Support, Still Gets Jail Time," Fox 26 Houston, January 3, 2014. http://www.myfoxhouston.com/story/24359680/2014/01/03/father-pays-outstanding-child-support-still-gets-jail-time#ixzz2pSVyXskk.
3. Murray A. Straus, "Women's Violence Toward Men Is a Serious Social Problem." In D.R. Loseke, R.J. Gelles, and M.M. Cavanaugh (Eds.), *Current Controversies on Family Violence*, 2nd Edition, Newbury Park: Sage Publications, 2005 55–77.
4. Email to the author from Joe, December 13, 2013.
5. "A tendency for the procedures and practices of particular institutions to operate in ways which result in certain social groups being advantaged or favoured and others being disadvantaged or devalued. This need not be the result of any conscious prejudice or discrimination but rather of the majority simply following existing rules or norms. Institutional racism and institutional sexism are the most common examples." From Oxford Reference at http://www.oxfordreference.com/view/10.1093/oi/authority.20110803100005347.
6. Email to the author from Shawn, December 25, 2013.
7. Katie Allison Granju, "Husband Want a Vasectomy? He'll Have to Get Your Permission," Babble.com, February 12, 2011, at http://www.babble.com/babble-voices/home-work/husband-want-a-vasectomy-hell-have-to-get-your-permission/.
8. Lu Fong, "Are Men Legally Required to Ask Their Spouse's Permission For a Vasectomy?" The Good Men Project, Feb-

196

ruary 23, 2011, at http://goodmenproject.com/newsroom/are
-men-legally-required-to-ask-their-spouses-permission-for
-a-vasectomy/.

9. William Saletan, "The Case Against Reproductive Freedom,"
Slate.com, January 27, 2014, at http://www.slate.com/blogs/
saletan/2014/01/27/ross_douthat_s_case_against_contra
ception_is_reproductive_choice_too_dangerous.html.

10. Letter to the author from Christian, January 1, 2014.

Introduction

1. Website at www.PJMedia.com.
2. See http://www.pjtv.com/?cmd=mpg&mpid=109.
3. 2012 American Foundation of Suicide Statistics, http://
www.afsp.org/index.cfm?fuseaction=home.viewPage&page_
ID=04ECB949-C3D9-5FFA-DA9C65C381BAAEC0.
4. "American Father Self-Immolates to Protest Against Family
Courts," *International Business Times*, June 17, 2011, http://
www.ibtimes.com/articles/164827/20110617/thomas-ball-
self-immolate-child-support.htm.
5. Helen Smith, "On Fire, but Blacked Out: The Thomas Ball
Story," *PJMedia* (blog), June 29, 2011, http://pjmedia.com/
blog/on-fire-but-blacked-out-the-thomas-ball-story/.
6. Helen Smith, "Going John Galt," *Dr. Helen* (blog), October
12, 2008, http://drhelen.blogspot.com/2008/10/going-john-
galt.html.
7. Ayn Rand, *Atlas Shrugged*, 50th Anniversary Edition, New
York: Signet, 1996.
8. Jennifer Burns, *Goddess of the Market: Ayn Rand and the American Right*. New York: Oxford University Press, 2009, 149.
9. Sophia Borland, "Business Man Sues British Airlines 'for
treating men like perverts,'" *Daily Mail Online*, January
16, 2010, http://www.dailymail.co.uk/news/article-1243625/
Businessman-Mirko-Fisher-sues-British-Airways-treating-
men-like-perverts.html?ITO=1490.
10. Warren Farrell, *The Myth of Male Power: Why Men Are the
Disposable Sex*, New York: Simon & Schuster, 1993.
11. Ibid., 369.
12. Ibid., 368. "Emphasis in original."

13. James Q. Wilson, "Angry About Inequality? Don't Blame the Rich," *Washington Post*, January 26, 2012, http://www.washingtonpost.com/opinions/angry-about-inequality-dont-blame-the-rich/2012/01/03/gIQA9S2fTQ_story.html.

Chapter 1. The Marriage Strike

1. Ernie, October 31, 2007 (7:33 a.m.) comment on Helen Smith, "Should Men Get Married?" *Dr. Helen* (blog), *PJMedia*, October 31, 2007, http://pjmedia.com/blog/ask_dr_helen_6/.

2. Kay Hymowitz, *Manning Up: How the Rise of Women Has Turned Men into Boys*, New York: Basic Books, 2011, 111.

3. Suzanne Venker, "The War on Men" FoxNews.com, November 26, 2012, http://www.foxnews.com/opinion/2012/11/24/war-on-men/?intcmp=features#ixzz2DeHfewS3.

4. Eduardo Porter and Michelle O'Donnell, "Facing Middle Age with No Degree, and No Wife," *New York Times*, August 6, 2006, http://www.nytimes.com/2006/08/06/us/06marry.html?pagewanted=all.

5. Betsy Stevenson, "Who's Getting Married? Education and Marriage Today and in the Past," Council on Contemporary Families, January 26, 2010, www.contemporaryfamilies.org/images/stories/homepage/orange_border/ccf012510.pdf.

6. Glenn Sacks and Dianna Thompson, "Have Anti-Father Family Court Policies Led to a Men's Marriage Strike?" *Philadelphia Inquirer*, July 5, 2002, found at http://www.ejfi.org/Civilization/Civilization-10.htm#strike.

7. Hymowitz, *Manning Up*.

8. Kathleen Parker, *Save the Males: Why Men Matter Why Women Should Care*, New York: Random House, 2008.

9. Michael Kimmel, *Guyland: The Perilous World Where Boys Become Men*, New York: Harper Collins, 2008.

10. Leonard Sax, *Boys Adrift: The Five Factors Driving the Growing Epidemic of Unmotivated Boys and Underachieving Young Men*, New York: Basic Books, 2007.

11. Richard Whitmire, *Why Boys Fail: Saving Our Sons from an Educational System That's Leaving Them Behind*, AMACOM, 2010.

12. Hymowitz, "Praise for Manning Up," *Manning Up*.

13. Jenna Goudreau, "Has the Rise of Women Turned Men into Boys?" *Forbes*, March 3, 2011, found at http://www.forbes.com/sites/jennagoudreau/2011/03/03/rise-of-women-turned-men-into-boys-manning-up-kay-hymowitz/.

14. Hymowitz, *Manning Up*, 118–121.

15. Hanna Rosin, *The End of Men and the Rise of Women*, New York: Penguin Group, 2012.

16. Jessica Bennett, "It's Not 'The End of Men' But They Are in Trouble," *The Daily Beast*, September 12, 2012, at http://www.thedailybeast.com/articles/2012/09/12/new-book-suggests-it-s-not-the-end-of-men-but-they-are-in-trouble.html.

17. Donna Britt, "The Rage Behind a Woman's Stare," *Washington Post*, January 29, 2012, found at http:www.washingtonpost.com/lifestyle/style.donna-britt-she-wears-the-death-look-well/2012/01/26/gIQAD1K9aQ_story.html?wpisrc-email-toafriend.

18. Cassie Shortsleeve, "The Sex Secret Live-In Girlfriends Know," *Men's Health News*, January 26, 2012, http://news.menshealth.com/sex-and-marriage/2012/01/26/.

19. Nanci Hellmich, "Gain a Spouse and You'll Likely Gain Some Pounds, Too," *USA Today*, October 23, 2007, http://usatoday30.usatoday.com/news/health/2007-10-22-marriage-weight_N.htm.

20. Shortsleeve, "The Sex Secret Live-In Girlfriends Know."

21. Ibid.

22. For instance, check out the "Beware of the Doghouse" from J.C. Penney at creativity-online.com/work/jc-penney-beware-of-the-doghouse/14501.

23. Lee Dye, "Why Are More Men Waiting to Marry?" ABC News, August 14 2011, http://abcnews.go.com/Technology/story?id=97920&page=1.

24. Porter and O'Donnell, "Facing Middle Age with No Degree, and No Wife," *New York Times*, August 6, 2006.

25. Ibid.

26. Joinson, A. "Causes and Implications of Disinhibition Behaviors on the Internet." In J. Gackenbach (Ed.), *Psychology and the Internet*, New York: Academic Press, 1998, 43–48.

27. Jack, January 19, 2006 (3:56 p.m.) comment on Helen Smith, "Marrying Well ... Make That, Why Marry?"

Dr. Helen (blog), January 17, 2006, http://drhelen.blogspot
.com/2006/01/marrying-wellmake-that-why-marry
.html#113770421180100813.

28. Helen Smith, "Marrying Well . . . Make That, Why Marry?"
January 17, 2006, http://drhelen.blogspot.com/2006/01/
marrying-well-make-that-why-marry.html.

29. Helen Smith, "Should Men Get Married?" *Dr. Helen* (blog),
PJMedia, October 31, 2007, http://pjmedia.com/blog/ask_
dr_helen_6/.

30. Anonymous, July 29, 2007 (1:16 a.m.) comment on Helen
Smith, "Marrying Well . . . Make That, Why Marry?"

31. Anonymous, April 7, 2007 (6:30 p.m.) comment on Helen
Smith, "Marrying Well . . . Make That, Why Marry?"

32. Anonymous, January 20, 2006 (11:10 a.m.) comment on
Helen Smith, "Marrying Well . . . Make That, Why Marry?"

33. Jack, January 16, 2006 (3:56 p.m.).

34. Barry, October 31, 2007 (9:32 a.m.) comment on Helen Smith,
"Should Men Get Married?" *Dr. Helen* (blog), *PJMedia*, October 31, 2007, http://pjmedia.com/blog/ask_dr_helen_6/.

35. Found at http://alphagameplan.blogspot.com/.

36. See examples from blogger Roissy at http://heartiste.word-
press.com/ or Athol Kay at http://www.marriedmansexlife
.com/.

37. James Taranto, "The American Shengnu: Why Charles Murray May Be Too Optimistic," *Wall Street Journal*, March 14,
2012, http://online.wsj.com/article/SB1000142405270230469
2804577281581288138216.html.

38. Vox Popoli, "Roissy and the Limits of Game," January 29,
2010, http://voxday.blogspot.com/2010/01/roissy-and-limits-
of-game.html.

39. Vox Day, February 21, 2012, "Alpha Game Demograph-
ics," *Alpha Game* (blog), http://alphagameplan.blogspot.
com/2012/02/alpha-game-demographics.html.

40. Author email interview with Vox Day, February 20, 2012.

41. James Taranto, "Girls Gone Hyper" *Wall Street Journal*, Best
of the Web, February 14, 2012, found at http://online.wsj
.com/article/SB100014240529702047953045772233423548502
00.html.

42. Jena Turner, "10 Female Celebrities with Highest Number

of Affairs," *Women Tribe.com*, http://www.womentribe.com/entertainment/10-female-celebrities-with-highest-number-of-affairs.html.

Chapter 2. My Body, My Choice—Your Body, No Choice

1. Paul Nathanson and Katherine K. Young, *Legalizing Misandry: From Public Shame to Systemic Discrimination Against Men*, Montreal: McGill-Queens University Press, 2006, 151.
2. Found at http://irregulartimes.com/mybodymychoice.html.
3. Warren Farrell, *The Myth of Male Power*, New York: Simon & Schuster, 1993, 36.
4. See Michelle Oberman, *Sex Lies and the Duty to Disclose*, 47 Ariz. L. Rev. 871 (2005); J. Terrell Mann, *Misrepresentation of Sterility or of Use of Birth Control*, 26 J. Fam. L. 623 (1988).
5. Nathanson and Young, *Legalizing Misandry*, 154–155.
6. Helen Smith, "Can a Man be Raped by a Woman?" *Dr. Helen* (blog), *PJ Media*, June 30, 2008, http://pjmedia.com/blog/ask-dr-helen-can-a-man-be-raped-by-a-woman/.
7. Higdon, Michael J., *Fatherhood by Conscription: Nonconsensual Insemination and the Duty of Child Support*, (February 14, 2011). University of Tennessee Legal Studies Research Paper No. 139. Available at Social Science Resource Network at http://ssrn.com/abstract=1761333 or http://dx.doi.org/10.2139/ssrn.1761333.
8. Cnty. of San Luis Obispo vs. Nathaniel J., 57 Cal. Rptr. 2d 843-44 (Ct. App.1996). at 844.
9. Higdon, *Fatherhood by Conscription*, 1–2.
10. Ibid., 2.
11. Farrell, *The Myth of Male Power*, 365. "Emphasis in original."
12. Donald C. Hubin, "Daddy Dilemmas: Untangling the Puzzles of Paternity," *Cornell Journal of Law and Public Policy* 13 (Fall 2003): 29–80, 51.
13. Higdon, *Fatherhood by Conscription*,13.
14. DCSE/Ester M.C. v. Mary L., No. 38812, 1994 WL 811732 (Del. Fam. Ct. Jan. 3, 1994) at *1.
15. Ibid, at *3.
16. Found at http://www.codemonkeyramblings.com/2008/12/

state-sanctioned-paternity-fraud-another-reason-why-men-
have-less-incentive-to-marry/.

17. Carnell Smith's website at http://www.paternityfraud.com/.

18. Fathers and Families is an excellent organization formerly
    run by men's rights activist Glenn Sacks and currently run
    by Dr. Ned Holstein, found at http://www.fathersandfamilies
    .org/.

19. Oliver Broudy, "Are You Raising Another Man's Child?"
    Men's Health Magazine, March 6, 2007, at http://www.mens
    health.com/best-life/fathers-and-kids-parenting-fraud.

20. Ibid, 1.

21. Ibid.

22. Ibid, 5.

23. Helen Smith, "How would you feel if you found out you were
    raising another man's child?" *Dr. Helen* (blog), *PJMedia*, Feb-
    ruary 14, 2012, http://pjmedia.com/drhelen/2012/02/14/how-
    would-you-feel-if-you-found-out-you-were-raising-another-
    mans-child/.

24. Ibid.

25. Joe in Houston, February 15, 2012 (4:10 p.m.), comment on
    Helen Smith, "How would you feel if you found out you were
    raising another man's child?"

26. Tiger6, February 15, 2012 (7:17 a.m.), comment on "If you
    found out tomorrow that your five-year-old son or daughter
    was not yours and had to pay 13 years of child support, how
    would you feel?" poll, http://poll.pollcode.com/zvkj_result?v.

27. Difster, February 15, 2012 (2:07 a.m.), comment on "If you
    found out tomorrow that your five-year-old son or daughter
    was not yours . . ." poll.

28. Old Guy, February 14, 2012 (11:55 p.m.), comment on "If you
    found out tomorrow that your five-year-old son or daughter
    was not yours . . ." poll.

29. Cthulhu, February 14, 2012 (8:18 p.m.), comment on "If you
    found out tomorrow that your five-year-old son or daughter
    was not yours . . ." poll.

30. TeeJaw, February 15, 2012 (11:31 a.m.), comment on "If you
    found out tomorrow that your five-year-old son or daughter
    was not yours . . ." poll.

31. PJTV interview with Stacey Campfield, December 24, 2008
    at http://www.pjtv.com/?cmd=mpg&mpid=109&load=1046.

32. Jesse Fox Mayshark, "What the Heck Is Wrong with Stacey Campfield?" *Metro Pulse*, September 29, 2010, http://www.metropulse.com/news/2010/sep/29/what-heck-wrong-stacey-campfield/.

33. Ibid.

34. Ibid.

35. Email exchange with Stacey Campfield, December 2, 2008.

36. Tina Marie Hodge v. Chadwick Craig No. 2009-00930-SC-R11-CV, (Filed in TN Oct. 1, 2012).

37. Stacey Campfield, October 12,2012, "Baby Daddy Ruling," *Camp4u* (blog), http://lastcar.blogspot.com/2012/10/baby-daddy-ruling.html.

38. Found at http://www.paternityfraud.com/2002-georgia-paternity-fraud-bill-hb369ap.html.

39. Found at Carnell Smith's website, http://www.carnellsmith.com/Media-Comments/.

40. Author interview with Carnell Smith, March 31, 2012.

41. Douglas Galbi, "Persons in Jail or in Prison for Child-Support Debt," *Purple Motes*, March 22, 2011, found at http://purplemotes.net/2011/03/22/persons-in-jail-for-child-support-debt/.

42. Tim S. Grall, "Custodial Mothers and Fathers and their Child Support: 2009," December 2011 found at http://www.census.gov/prod/2011pubs/p60-240.pdf.

43. Mike Brunker, "Unable to Pay Child Support, Poor Parents Land Behind Bars," Sept. 12, 2011, *MSNBC*, http://www.msnbc.msn.com/id/44376665/ns/us_crime_and_courts/t/unable-pay-child-support-poor-parents-land-behind-bars/.

44. Ibid.

45. Carl Bialek, "Data on Arrest Records Aren't Always on the Book," *Wall Street Journal*, November 2009, http://online.wsj.com/article/SB125851115456653127.html.

46. See Glenn Sacks, "Passport rules unfair to child support debtors" at http://glennsacks.com/blog/?page_id=1140.

Chapter 3. The College Strike

1. Author email interview with Christina Hoff Sommers, March 6, 2012.

2. Christina Hoff Sommers, *The War Against Boys: How Misguided Feminism Is Harming Our Young Men*, New York: Simon & Schuster, 2000, 30.

3. U.S. Department of Education, National Center for Education Statistics. (2011). *Digest of Education Statistics, 2010* (NCES 2011-015), Table 198, http://nces.ed.gov/fastfacts/display.asp?id=98.

4. Ibid.

5. Kay Hymowitz, *Manning Up*, Basic Books, New York, 2011, 50–51.

6. U.S. Department of Education, "Table 268: Degrees Conferred by Degree Granting Institutions by Level of Degree and Sex of Student," Digest of Education Statistics, http://nces.ed.gov/programs/digest/d09/tables/dt09_268.asp.

7. Alex Williams, "The New Math on Campus," February 5, 2010, http://www.nytimes.com/2010/02/07/fashion/07campus.html?pagewanted=all&_r=0.

8. Ibid.

9. Sommers, *The War Against Boys*, 14.

10. Ibid., 44.

11. Metropolitan Life Insurance Company, *The American Teacher, 1997: Examining Gender Issues in Public Schools.*

12. Sommers, *The War Against Boys*, 29.

13. Ibid., citing *U.S. Department of Education*, National Center for Education Statistics, The Condition of Education 1998, 262.

14. Author email interview with Sommers, March 6, 2012.

15. Lucy Sheriff, "Female Teachers Give Male Pupils Lower Marks, Claims Study," February 16, 2012, at http://www.huffingtonpost.co.uk/2012/02/16/female-teachers-give-male_n_1281236.html.

16. Robyn Dawes, "The Social Usefulness of Self-Esteem: A Skeptical View," *The Harvard Mental Health Letter*, Volume 4, October 1998, 5.

17. Helen Smith, *The Scarred Heart: Understanding and Identifying Kids who Kill*, Callisto Publishing, 2000.

18. Author email interview with Sommers, March 12, 2012.

19. Michael Greenstone and Adam Looney, "Have Earnings Actually Declined?" *Brookings Institution*, The Hamilton Project, March 4, 2011.http://www.brookings.edu/opinions/2011/0304_jobs_greenstone_looney.aspx.

20. Ibid.

21. Michael Greenstone and Adam Looney, "The Problem with Men: A Look at Long-term Employment Trends," The Brookings Institution, December 3, 2010, http://www.brookings.edu/opinions/2010/1203_jobs_greenstone_looney.aspx.

22. John Ydstie, "Why Some Men Earn Less than They Did 40 Years Ago," NPR, September 17, 2011, http://www.npr.org/2011/09/17/140554967/median-male-workers-income-lower-than-in-1973.

23. Hymowitz, *Manning Up*, 51–52.

24. Robert Weissberg, "The White Male Shortage on Campus," February 12, 2012, *Minding the Campus* website, http://www.mindingthecampus.com/originals/2012/02/the_academys_shortage_of_white_males.html.

25. Author email interview with Christina Hoff Sommers, March 6, 2012.

26. Jim, February 14, 2012 (6:04 p.m.), comment on Robert Weissberg, "The White Male Shortage on Campus," February 12, 2012, *Minding the Campus* website, http://www.mindingthecampus.com/originals/2012/02/the_academys_shortage_of_white_males.html.

27. Glenn Sacks, "Why Males Don't Go to College," *Mensight Magazine*, 2002, found at http://glennsacks.com/blog/?page_id=2180.

28. Email to the author on March 10, 2012.

29. Email to the author on March 11, 2012.

30. Email to the author on March 10, 2012.

31. Email to the author on March 14, 2012.

32. Peter Berkowitz, "College Rape Accusations and the Presumption of Male Guilt," *Wall Street Journal*, August 20, 2011, http://online.wsj.com/article/SB10001424053111903596904576516232905230642.html.

33. For more on this case, read Stuart Taylor and K.C. Johnson, *Until Proven Innocent: Political Correctness and the Shameful Injustices of the Duke Lacrosse Rape Case*, Thomas Dunne Books, September 4, 2007.

34. Berkowitz, "College Rape Accusations and Presumption of Male Guilt."

35. Christina Hoff Sommers, "In Making Campuses Safe for Women, a Travesty of Justice for Men," *Chronicle of Higher*

Education, June 5, 2011, http://chronicle.com/article/In-Mak
ing-Campuses-Safe-for/127766/.

36. Ibid.
37. See *The Futurist* blog at http://www.singularity2050
.com/2010/01/the-misandry-bubble.html.

Chapter 4. Why Does Dad Stay in the Basement?

1. Rachel Rabbit White, "Girl Talk: Why Am I Afraid of
Men?" *The Frisky*, January 27, 2012, http://www.thefrisky
.com/2012-01-27/girl-talk-why-am-i-scared-of-men/#un
defined.
2. Kathleen Parker, *Save the Males: Why Men Matter Why
Women Should Care*, Random House: New York, 2008, 36.
3. Sophie Borland, "Businessman sues BA 'for treating men
like perverts,'" *Daily Mail*, January 16, 2010, http://www
.dailymail.co.uk/news/article-1243625/Businessman-Mirko-
Fischer-sues-British-Airwars-treating-men-like-perverts.html.
4. Sandy Maple, "Men afraid of being labeled as pedophiles," Parent Dish, June 1, 2007, http://www.parentdish
.com/2007/06/01/men-afraid-of-being-labeled-pedophiles/.
5. Wendy McElroy, "Did Pedophilia Hysteria Cause Child's
Death?" FoxNews.com, April 4, 2006, http://www.foxnews
.com/story/0,2933,190586,00.html.
6. Ibid.
7. Ibid.
8. Maple, "Men afraid of being labeled as pedophiles."
9. Iggy, June 4, 2007 (8:53 a.m.), comment on Sandy Maple,
"Men afraid of being labeled as pedophiles."
10. NV, June 1, 2007 (5:23 p.m.), comment on Sandy Maple,
"Men afraid of being labeled as pedophiles."
11. Found at http://tedxwomen.org/speakers/jennifer-siebel-
newsom/.
12. Miss Representation website at http://www.missrepresenta
tion.org/about-us/.
13. Ibid.
14. You can see the glam picture at the filmmaker's website at
http://www.jennifersiebelnewsom.com/ I have to agree that
this woman does seem to put a big emphasis on beauty and

seems to have made a living at it, while simultaneously castigating those in the media who place too much emphasis on beauty. While I get her point, if she is also buying into the hype, what kind of role model is she for young girls?

15. U.S. Census Bureau, Family Living Arrangements, 2011, at http://www.census.gov/hhes/families/data/cps2011.html.

16. Lauren Cox, "The Mistrusted Male Teacher," ABC News, August 28, 2008 at http://abcnews.go.com/Health/story?id=5670187&page=1#.UKEkYYXgK3U.

17. Kathleen Parker, p. 20, discussing the work of Jim Macnamara, author of Media and Male Identity.

18. "Men become the main target in the new gender wars," University of Western Sydney, November 27, 2006., at http://www.physorg.com/news83863660.html.

19. Kathleen Parker, p. 20, quoting from Dr. Jim Macnamara in an online interview; University of Western Sydney, November 27, 2006, www.physorg.com/news83863660.html.

20. Ibid.

21. Parker, 18.

22. Ibid.

23. Helen Smith, "How Many Negative Images of Men Do You See on TV in Ten Minutes?" *PJ Media*, March 22, 2012, http://pjmedia.com/lifestyle/2012/03/23/why-do-ads-that-diss-women-get-removed-while-ads-that-diss-men-are-funny/.

24. Richard Ricardo, March 22, 2012 (5:26 a.m.), comment on Helen Smith, "How Many Negative Images of Men Do you See on TV in Ten Minutes?"

25. Tex Taylor, March 22, 2012 (1:32 p.m.), comment on Helen Smith, "How Many Negative Images of Men Do You See on TV in Ten Minutes?"

26. Mac, March 22, 2012 (3:20 p.m.), comment on Helen Smith, "How Many Negative Images of Men Do You See on TV in Ten Minutes?"

27. Bob, March 25, 2012 (8:19 a.m.), comment on Helen Smith, "How Many Negative Images of Men Do You See on TV in Ten Minutes?"

28. Playstead, January 11, 2010 (3:09 a.m.), comment on Brett McKay, "The Decline of Male Space," *The Art of Manliness* website, January 10. 2010, http://artofmanliness

.com/2010/01/10/the-decline-of-male-space/comment-page-1/#comments.

29. Brett McKay, "The Decline of Male Space," The Art of Manliness website, January 10. 2010, http://artofmanliness .com/2010/01/10/the-decline-of-male-space/comment-page-1/#comments.

30. Ibid.

31. Ibid.

32. Charles Murray, *Coming Apart: The State of White America, 1960–2010.* Crown Forum: New York, 2012, 239–240.

33. Mary Jo Rapini, "Why He Needs a Man Cave," *Your Tango .com,* March 6, 2012, http://www.yourtango.com/experts/mary-jo-rapini/man-cave-prevents-communication-problems.

Chapter 5. Why It Matters

1. Rich Lowry, "Dude, Where's My Lifeboat?" *National Review Online,* January 17, 2012, http://www.nationalreview.com/articles/288253/dude-where-s-my-lifeboat-rich-lowry.

2. Wikipedia, *Costa Concordia* disaster, http://en.wikipedia.org/wiki/Costa_Concordia_disaster.

3. Silvia Ognibene, "Prosecutors target cruise ship captain, Costa executives," Reuters, February 23, 2012. Archived from the original on February 28, 2012, http://www.webcitation .org/65mQ7BysG. Retrieved February 28, 2012.

4. Lowry, "Dude, Where's My Lifeboat?"

5. Rosin, *The End of Men,* 149.

6. Ibid., 4–5.

7. Berhanu Alemayehu and Kenneth E. Warner, "The Lifetime Distribution of Health Care Costs," Health Serv Res. 2004 June; 39(3): 627–642 at http://www.ncbi.nlm.nih.gov/pmc/articles/PMC1361028/.

8. Douglas Laycock, "Vicious Stereotypes in Polite Society," 8 Constitutional Commentary 395, 1991, http://www.saf.org/lawreviews/laycock1.htm.

9. Wendy Brown, "Guns, Cowboys, Philadelphia Mayors, and Civic Republicanism: On Sanford Levinson's The Embarrassing Second Amendment," *Yale Law Journal,* 99 Yale L.J. 661 (1989), http://saf.org/LawReviews/BrownW1.html.

10. Laycock, "Vicious Stereotypes in Polite Society."
11. Rahim Kanani, "The Need to Create a White House Council on Boys to Men," *Forbes*, September 5, 2011, http://www.forbes.com/sites/rahimkanani/2011/09/05/the-need-to-create-a-white-house-council-on-boys-to-men/.
12. Chateau Heartiste, "Charles Murray's One-Sided Shaming," March 19, 2012, *Chateau Heartiste* (blog), http://heartiste.wordpress.com/2012/03/19/charles-murrays-one-sided-shaming/.
13. Lisa Belkin, "Why Men Opting-Out Should Make You Angry," *Huffington Post Women* (blog), March 23, 2012, http://www.huffingtonpost.com/lisa-belkin/men-opting-out_b_1375355.html.
14. Rudy in la, March 27, 2012 (12:08 p.m.) comment on Lisa Belkin, "Why Men Opting-Out Should Make You Angry."
15. Belkin, "Why Men Opting-Out Should Make You Angry."
16. Charles Murray, "Why Economics Can't Explain Our Cultural Divide," *Wall Street Journal*, March 16, 2012, http://online.wsj.com/article/SB10001424052702304692804577281582403394206.html?mod=WSJ_LifeStyle_Lifestyle_5.
17. Chateau Heartiste. "Charles Murray's One-Sided Shaming."
18. Toby Harnden, "Are you better off? Just 96,000 jobs added in August as 368,000 people LEAVE the workforce in bleak employment report dealing blow to Obama re-election hopes." *The Daily Mail*, September 7, 2012.
19. Helen Smith, "Why is the participation of men in the workplace so low?" *Dr. Helen* (blog), *PJ Media*. September 7, 2012, http://pjmedia.com/drhelen/2012/09/07/why-is-the-participation-rate-of-men-in-the-workforce-so-low/.
20. JKB, September 7, 2012 (10:02 am) comment on Helen Smith, "Why is the participation of men in the workplace so low?"
21. Oso Pardo, September 7, 2012 (10:15 a.m.), comment on Helen Smith, "Why is the participation of men in the workplace so low?"
22. Vic, September 7, 2012 (1:02 p.m.), comment on Helen Smith, "Why is the participation of men in the workplace so low?"
23. Tobytylersf, September 7, 2012 (3:50 p.m.) comment on Helen Smith, "Why is the participation of men in the workplace so low?"
24. Jason DeParle and Sabrina Taverni, "For Women Under

30, Most Births Occur Outside Marriage," *New York Times*, February 17, 2012, http://www.nytimes.com/2012/02/18/us/ for-women-under-30-most-births-occur-outside-marriage .html?_r=1.

25. Shari Roan, "Drop in U.S. birth rate is the biggest in 30 years," March 31, 2011, *Los Angeles Times*, http://articles.latimes .com/2011/mar/31/news/la-heb-us-birth-rate-falls-2011 0331.

26. Jim Macnamara, *Media and Male Identity: The Making and Re-making of Men* (New York, Palgrave Macmillan, 2006), 179– 180.

27. Ibid., 179.

28. *Sydney Morning Herald, Good Weekend* magazine, February 12, 2005, letter to the editor, 8.

29. Warren Farrell, *The Myth of Male Power*, New York: Simon & Schuster: 1993, 370.

Chapter 6. Fighting Back, Going Galt or Both?

1. Andrea Cornwall, "Boys and men must be included in the conversation on equality," *Poverty Matters Blog, Guardian*, March 21, 2012. http://www.guardian.co.uk/global-develop ment/poverty-matters/2012/mar/21/boys-men-part-of- equality-conversation?INTCMP=SRCH.

2. Macnamara, *Media and Male Identity*, 149.

3. Richard Driscoll, *You Still Don't Understand*, Knoxville, Tenn.: Westside Psychology, 2009.

4. Dale Carnegie, *Quick and Easy Way to Effective Speaking*, New Win Pub., 1973.

5. Robert Heinlein, *Take Back Your Government*, Baen, July 1, 1992.

6. David Horowitz, *How to Beat the Democrats and Other Subver- sive Ideas*, Spence Publishing Company, 2003.

7. Saul Alinsky, *Rules for Radicals*, Vintage, October 23, 1989.

8. http://www.thefrisky.com/relationships/.

9. http://www.yourtango.com/what-men-think.

10. Author email interview with Glenn Sacks, April 9, 2012.

11. Phone interview, March 31,2012 with Carnell Smith PfV Emancipationist / Consultant. His signature line is "If the

genes don't fit . . . you must acquit" and his website is www
.CarnellSmith.com.

12. Biography of Carnell Smith at http://www.carnellsmith.com/
Biography/.

13. Ibid.

14. Email interview with Carnell Smith, April 2, 2012.

15. http://en.wikipedia.org/wiki/Coverture.

16. Paul Thompson, "Unwitting father sues fertility clinic after
his girlfriend 'stole his sperm and got pregnant with twins
via IVF'—then sued him for child support" *Daily Mail*,
November 23, 2011, http://www.dailymail.co.uk/news/
article-2065293/New-father-Joe-Pressil-sues-fertility-clinic-
girlfriend-stole-sperm-got-pregnant-gave-birth-twins-IVF
.html.

17. State v. Frisard, 694 So.2d 1032, 1035 (LA. CT. App. 1997).

18. Dean Cardell, "Sperm-Jackers: The Five Types," *AskMen*
.com, http://www.askmen.com/dating/curtsmith_400/407_
sperm-jackers-the-5-types.html.

19. Michael Walzer, *Just and Unjust Wars: A Moral Argument with
Historical Illustrations* (2000).

20. Mission statement at the FIRE website at http://thefire.org/
about/mission/.

21. Email interview from April 2, 2012.

22. Stephenlclark, April 6, 2012 (2:20 p.m.), comment on
Helen Smith, "How Should Men 'Go Galt' in a female-
centered society?," *Dr. Helen* (blog), *PJ Media*, April 6,
2012, http://pjmedia.com/drhelen/2012/04/06/how-should-
men-go-galt-in-a-female-centered-society/.

23. JKB, April 7, 2012 (7:13 a.m.) comment on Helen Smith,
"How Should Men 'Go Galt' in a female-centered society?"

24. Eric R., April 6, 2012 (2:59 p.m.) comment on Helen Smith,
"How Should Men 'Go Galt' in a female-centered society?"

25. Armageddon Rex, April 6, 2012 (11:24 p.m.) comment on
Helen Smith, "How Should Men 'Go Galt' in a female-
centered society?"

26. J. Gottman and R. Levenson, "Assessing the Role of Emotion
in Marriage," *Behavioral Assessment*, 8, 1986; 31–48; Gottman
and Levenson, 1988, J. Gottman, "How Marriages Change."
In G. Paterson (ed.), *Family Social Interaction: Content and*

Methodological Issues in the Study of Aggression and Depression (Hillsdale, NY: Erlbaum, 1990), 75–101.

27. Richard Driscoll, *You Still Don't Understand*, Knoxville, Tenn.: Westside Psychology, 2009, 48.
28. Ibid.
29. http://www.orgformen.org/4436.html.
30. Scott Adams, *The Dilbert Future*, Harper Collins, New York, 1998, 108.
31. Author Interview at PJTV with Glenn Sacks, December 10, 2008. http://www.pjtv.com/?cmd=mpg&mpid=109&load =981.

Conclusion

1. Christina Hoff Sommers, discussing the work of Camille Paglia in *The War Against Boys*, New York: Simon & Schuster, 2000, 63–64.

Index